ZEND

PHP Certification

STUDY GUIDE

Zend Technologies

Sams Publishing, 800 East 96th Street, Indianapolis, Indiana 46240 USA

Zend PHP Certification Study Guide

International Standard Book Number: 0-672-32709-0

Library of Congress Catalog Card Number: 2004093764

Printed in the United States of America

First Printing: July 2004

07 06 05 04   4 3 2 1

Trademarks

Warning and Disclaimer

Bulk Sales

Sams Publishing offers excellent discounts on this book when ordered in quantity for bulk purchases or special sales. For more information, please contact

U.S. Corporate and Government Sales
1-800-382-3419
corpsales@pearsontechgroup.com

For sales outside of the U.S., please contact

International Sales
1-317-428-3341
international@pearsontechgroup.com

Acquisitions Editor
Shelley Johnston

Development Editor
Damon Jordan

Managing Editor
Charlotte Clapp

Project Editor
George E. Nedeff

Copy Editor
Rhonda Tinch-Mize

Indexer
Chris Barrick

Proofreader
Leslie Joseph

Technical Editor
Sara Golemon

Publishing Coordinator
Vanessa Evans

Multimedia Developer
Dan Scherf

Book Designer
Gary Adair

Page Layout
Kelly Maish

Contents at a Glance

Table of Contents

About the Authors

Stuart Herbert has designed and implemented solutions for major companies such as Eurostar, Vodafone, and HP, and has been the lead maintainer of the Generic NQS project since 1994. A former systems manager with Orange UK, Stuart is currently one of the developers for Gentoo Linux, where he looks after Gentoo's installer for web-based packages.

Daniel Kushner is the director of training and certification at Zend Technologies. As director of training and certification, Daniel is responsible for the Zend PHP Certification program. In addition to designing the certification program, he developed the Zend PHP Training program, which provides the necessary study guide and classes to help PHP developers become Zend PHP certified. As part of the program, Daniel also initiates and maintains business relationships and partnerships with worldwide PHP training facilities. Prior to Zend Technologies, Daniel was a senior software engineer at DynamicLogic, responsible for developing integrated research recruitment solutions used in name brand websites including Yahoo!, AOL, and Lycos. Previously, he was a PHP freelancer, developing front and backend web applications, including e-commerce integration, member services and personalization, auction management, email delivery systems, and online file manipulation services for companies such as MTV, Arista, Viacom Outdoor, Accuweather, and Dell Computer Corporation. While freelancing, Daniel was also a PHP training instructor, where he worked with developers from highly acclaimed universities such as Harvard and Columbia and with companies such as Google, *The New York Times*, and the American Museum of Natural History.

George Schlossnagle is a principal at OmniTI Computer Consulting, a Maryland-based tech company specializing in high-volume web and email systems. Before joining OmniTI, George lead technical operations at several high-profile community websites, where he developed experience managing PHP in very large enterprise environments. George is a frequent contributor to the PHP community. His work can be found in the PHP core, as well as in the PEAR and PECL extension repositories. George also writes prolifically on PHP. He is the author of *Advanced PHP Programming* (Developers Library, 2004), as well as numerous articles for both print and online journals. He served as a subject matter expert for the Zend PHP Certification exam.

Chris Shiflett is a frequent contributor to the PHP community and one of the leading security experts in the field. His solutions to security problems are often used as points of reference, and these solutions are showcased in his talks at conferences such as ApacheCon and the O'Reilly Open Source Convention and his articles in publications such as *PHP Magazine* and *php|architect*. "Security Corner," his monthly column for *php|architect*, is the industry's first and foremost PHP security column. Chris is the author of the *HTTP Developer's Handbook* (Sams Publishing) and *PHP Security* (O'Reilly and Associates). In order to help bolster the strength of the PHP community, he is also leading an effort to create a PHP community site at PHPCommunity.org. Chris is also a subject matter expert for the Zend PHP Certification Exam.

Björn Schotte is a German PHP veteran. He co-founded the first German-speaking portal for PHP topics in early 1999, co-organized the first worldwide PHP conference, and has been editor-in-chief of *PHP Magazin* since 2001. He also co-founded ThinkPHP, Germany's No. 1 PHP solution company dealing mainly with large PHP applications for clients such as HypoVereinsbank, Sixt, Lycos Europe, E.ON, Cap Gemini, Ernst & Young, and others. His company now consists of a team of more than 15 people, including PHP core developers. Among his other accomplishments, he has beta-tested the MySQL Core Certification Program, is a well-known speaker at conferences such as CeBit Systems and LinuxTag where he promotes PHP in the enterprise, and has taught over 250 people in his PHP courses since 2000. You can reach him at schotte@mayflower.de. His company's website is at http://www.thinkphp.de/.

Marco Tabini is the publisher of *php|architect* (http://www.phparch.com), the premier magazine for PHP professionals, and has worked on websites for clients ranging from small startup operations to the Fortune 500s. Despite having been an IT industry professional for the last fifteen years, he still manages to maintain a reasonable level of sanity— at least most of the time. Marco is also a subject matter expert for the Zend PHP Certification Exam.

We Want to Hear from You!

As the reader of this book, *you* are our most important critic and commentator. We value your opinion and want to know what we're doing right, what we could do better, what areas you'd like to see us publish in, and any other words of wisdom you're willing to pass our way.

You can email or write me directly to let me know what you did or didn't like about this book—as well as what we can do to make our books stronger.

Please note that I cannot help you with technical problems related to the topic of this book, and that due to the high volume of mail I receive, I might not be able to reply to every message.

When you write, please be sure to include this book's title and author as well as your name and phone or email address. I will carefully review your comments and share them with the author and editors who worked on the book.

Email: opensource@samspublishing.com
Mail: Mark Taber
        Associate Publisher
        Sams Publishing
        800 East 96th Street
        Indianapolis, IN 46240 USA

Reader Services

For more information about this book or others from Sams Publishing, visit our website at www.samspublishing.com. Type the ISBN (0672327090) or the title of the book in the Search box to find the book you're looking for.

Foreword

PHP has grown a lot since its inception in 1997. PHP 4, released in May 2000, gained popularity and is already installed on more than a quarter of the Internet Web servers in the world—more than any other Web platform in existence as of mid-2003. Top-notch performance, the availability of good development tools such as the Zend Studio, and the explosive growth in availability of extension support for any third-party library or information store you can imagine have helped PHP become the best platform for developing and deploying Web applications.

With each passing month, it is becoming even more difficult to call PHP the "hidden gem of the Web." It is still a gem all right, but hidden? No longer. High profile companies, such as Lufthansa, Yahoo!, and Electronic Arts are now using PHP extensively, giving PHP a corporate "stamp of approval" for those who were waiting for one. An increasing number of companies are joining them every day, disproving those who say that PHP is not ready for the enterprise. With PHP 5, this trend is likely to continue even more rapidly.

As the scope of PHP widens, and as larger companies hire PHP personnel, they need to have a standard, reliable way of assessing one's abilities and capabilities with PHP. Moreover, the need for PHP developers to have an "official blessing" of their PHP skills is on the rise as the market becomes more competitive. The Zend PHP Certification program is aimed at providing a solution for both these companies and developers by providing a standard, objective, and comprehensive measurement of one's PHP skills.

This is exactly where this book comes into the picture. *Zend PHP Certification Study Guide* has been written by some of the same people who designed the Zend PHP Certification. It goes over all the topics that are required by the certification, placing an emphasis on the things that you need to keep in mind in order to pass the certification exam successfully. It is a must have for anybody planning to become a Zend Certified PHP Engineer—at least those who don't enjoy retaking exams.

Good luck with your test!

Andi Gutmans
Co-founder and
Vice President of Technology
Zend Technologies

Zeev Suraski
Co-founder and
Chief Technology Officer
Zend Technologies

Introduction

IF YOU'RE READING THIS BOOK, you've probably made a decision that becoming a Zend Certified Engineer is an important step in your career. And, indeed, it might well be—the certification exam will test your knowledge of PHP in many areas, ranging from the basics to the more complex topics. As PHP's adoption grows inside the enterprise, being certified can mean that you will have an edge when that dream job comes along!

The exam was designed by a number of well-known people in the PHP community in collaboration with experts in the field of computer-assisted testing. They approached it with a simple set of goals:

- Test the level of PHP knowledge of the candidate without prejudice to other technologies
- Use a set of testing questions that reflect real-world scenarios as accurately as possible
- Avoid questions that rely on a person's understanding of the language rather than his or her understanding of PHP and its related programming techniques

It's very important to understand these points as you approach your studies, as well as the exam itself, in particular when it comes to testing technologies that are used in conjunction with PHP. The test authors decided that, rather than relying on assumptions as to what other technologies a PHP programmer is likely to use in his or her daily job, the exam should focus on PHP itself and on those topics that a developer deals with often without any ties to a particular product.

Thus, although you will probably encounter one or more questions about database development during your exam, they will not be linked to a particular DBMS, such as MySQL or Oracle. Rather, they will deal with the general concepts of database programming and the standard SQL language.

What Does This Guide Cover?

The *Zend PHP Certification Study Guide* covers every topic that is part of the exam. It was developed by some of the very same authors who designed the exam's questions and was thoroughly reviewed to ensure that it provides every bit of information required to cover each subject appropriately.

One thing that this book is *not* is a PHP development tutorial or a reference book on the language and its extensions. Our goal in developing the guide is to provide you with a study aid that can help you focus on those topics that you will be questioned on during the exam. It is not a substitute for your experience as a PHP programmer in the real world, and it does not provide you with a "magic bullet" that will make you pass the test if you have never written a line of code in your life.

Remember that this book—and the certification guide—are based on PHP 4. This is essential, particularly when it comes to object-oriented programming, where the differences between PHP 4 and PHP 5 are very pronounced. Whatever you read in this book, as well as anything that shows up in a question at the exam, does not take PHP 5 into account *whatsoever.*

Many of the questions in the exam have been designed so that they mimic scenarios that you are likely to encounter in real life. Many of them involve the practical analysis of snippets of PHP code that might contain bugs or that might rely on PHP's particular behavior in order to reach a particular goal that is not immediately obvious.

These are not trick questions—they are designed to determine how well you understand the unique way in which PHP works so that, when a similar problem occurs in real life, you will be able to tackle it properly and efficiently.

We have designed this guide along the same lines. Although you will find a good amount of theory among the pages of this book, it will always be presented to you with an eye to its practical applications. In addition, each chapter includes a set of sample questions that are similar in structure to the ones you will find at the exam (although they are not the same, of course).

In line with our goal of giving you all the tools you need to successfully pass the exam, we thought you might also want to know what taking the exam is like. Chapter 13, "Getting Ready for the Certification Exam," discusses what to expect when you go to the certification center and how the exam works.

How Is the Guide Organized?

We intended the book to be read as a tutorial, rather than a reference. As such, the best way is to start with Chapter 1, "The Basics of PHP," and move your way to the end, as each chapter introduces new concepts by building on the information provided by the chapters that precede it.

While reading the guide, it's useful to remember that you are preparing for an exam. Read each section carefully and try to remember not only the essential points, but also those elements that might be useful while you're trying to tackle the exam.

If you already have experience in PHP development—as you probably will if you intend to take the exam—you might think that some of the topics we have covered in the guide are quite basic—and, to some extent, they are. However, they are covered from the point of view of the exam, and this means that you might discover some facts that you are not aware of because you have not encountered a real-life scenario in which they are relevant, but that might well show up in a question during your test.

Finally, don't forget to peruse the sample questions that you can find at the end of each chapter. As we mentioned earlier, they are similar in structure (although not in content) to the real ones, and they rely heavily on the proper analysis of practical sample code. Answering them can help you not only to determine how well your studies are progressing, but also to familiarize yourself with the way the questions are phrased in the exam.

Other Resources You Might Want to Consult

As we mentioned at the beginning of this introduction, there is no substitute for experience when it comes to passing the exam. You'll find that very few questions are of a didactical nature and that most require some practical steps in order to find the right answer.

Although this guide covers all the topics that are part of the exam, you might want to examine some of the subjects in more depth. The best resource for this purpose is the PHP Manual, which you can find online at http://www.php.net or through your local PHP mirror. In fact, it's probably a good idea to keep the manual handy while you're reading this book and refer to it for additional information on a specific topic. Simply remember that the manual covers all versions of PHP, whereas this guide and the exam are specific to PHP 4.

The Basics of PHP

PHP IS THE MOST POPULAR WEB-DEVELOPMENT language in the world. According to estimates compiled in April 2004, there are over fifteen million unique domains—and almost two million unique IPs—on the World Wide Web that reside on servers where PHP is supported and used.

The term "PHP" is actually a "recursive acronym" that stands for *PHP: Hypertext Preprocessor*. It might look a bit odd, but it is quite clever, if you think of it. PHP is a "scripting language"—a language intended for interpretation and execution rather than compilation such as, for example, C.

The fact that PHP is interpreted and not compiled, however, does not mean that it is incapable of meeting the demands of today's highly intensive web environments—in fact, a properly written PHP script can deliver incredibly high performance and power.

Terms You'll Need to Understand

- Language and Platform
- Language construct
- Data type
- Opening and closing tags
- Expression
- Variable
- Operation and operator precedence
- Conditional structures
- Iteration and Loops
- Functions
- Variable variables and variable functions

Techniques You'll Need to Master

- Creating a script
- Entering PHP mode
- Handling data types
- Type casting and type juggling
- Creating statements
- Creating operations and expressions
- Writing functions
- Handling conditional statements
- Handling loops

Language and Platform

The two biggest strengths of PHP are its simplicity and the incredible set of functionality that it provides. As a language, it incorporates C's elegant syntax without the hassle of memory and pointer management, as well as Perl's powerful constructs—without the complexity often associated with Perl scripts.

As a platform, PHP provides a powerful set of functions that cover a multitude of different needs and capabilities. Programmers who work on commercial platforms such as Microsoft ASP often marvel at the arsenal of functionality that a PHP developer has at his fingertips without the need to purchase or install anything other than the basic interpreter package. What's more, PHP is also *extensible* through a set of well-defined C APIs that make it easy for anyone to add more functionality to it as needed.

You have probably noticed that we have made a distinction between "language" and "platform." By the former, we mean PHP proper—the body of syntactical rules and constructs that make it possible to create a set of commands that can be executed in a particular sequence. The latter, on the other hand, is a term that we use to identify those facilities that make it possible for the language to perform actions such as communicating with the outside, sending an email, or connecting to a database.

The certification exam verifies your knowledge on both the language and the platform—after all, a good programmer needs to know how to write code *and* how to use all the tools at his disposal. Therefore, it is important that you acquaint yourself with both aspects of PHP development in order to successfully pass the exam.

Getting Started

The basic element of a PHP application is the *script*. A PHP script contains a number of commands that the PHP interpreter reads, parses, and executes.

Because PHP is designed to manipulate text files—such as HTML documents—and output them, the process of mixing hard-coded textual content and PHP code is facilitated by the fact that unless you tell it otherwise, the PHP interpreter considers the contents of the script file as plain text and outputs them as they are.

It's only when you explicitly indicate that you are embedding PHP code inside a file that the interpreter goes to work and starts parsing and executing commands. This is done by using a special set of *opening* and *closing tags*. In part because of historical reasons and in order to promote maximum flexibility, PHP supports three different sets of tags:

- PHP opening (`<?php`) and closing (`?>`) tags
- HTML-style tags (`<script language="php">` and `</script>`)
- "Short" tags: `<?` and `?>`
- "ASP-style" tags: `<%` and `%>`

The full PHP tags are always available to a script, whereas short tags and ASP-style tags might or might not be available to your script, depending on how the particular installation of the PHP interpreter used to execute it is configured. This is made necessary by the fact that short tags can interfere with XML documents, whereas ASP-style tags can interfere with other languages that can be used in conjunction with PHP in a chain of preprocessors that manipulate a file multiple times before it is outputted.

Let's take a look at the following sample PHP script:

```
<html>
<head>
<title>
    This is a sample document
</title>
<body>
    <?php
        echo 'This is some sample text';
    ?>
</body>
</html>
```

As you can see, this document looks exactly like a normal HTML page until the interpreter hits the `<?php` tag, which indicates that text following the tag should be interpreted as PHP commands and executed.

Right after the opening tag, we see a line of PHP code, which we'll examine in detail later on, followed by the `?>` closing tag. After the interpreter sees the closing tag, it stops trying to parse PHP commands and simply outputs the text as it appears without any change. Note that, as long as your copy of PHP has been configured to support more than one type of opening and closing tags, you *can* mix and match opening and closing tags from different families—for example, `<?php echo 'a' %>` would be a valid script. From a practical perspective, however, doing so would be pointless and confusing—definitely not a good programming practice.

Naturally, you can switch between plain-text and PHP execution mode at any point during your script and as long as you remember to balance your tags—that is, to close any tags you open, you can switch an arbitrary number of times.

The Special `<?= ?>` Tags

A special set of tags, `<?=` and `?>`, can be used to output the value of an expression directly to the browser (or, if you're not running PHP in a web environment to the standard output). They work by forcing PHP to evaluate the expression they contain and they output its value. For example,

```
<?= "This is an expression" ?>
```

Scripts and Files

It's important to note that there isn't necessarily a one-to-one correspondence between scripts and files—in fact, a script could be made up of an arbitrary number of files, each containing one or more portions of the code that must be executed. Clearly, this means that you can write portions of code so that they can be used by more than one script, such as library, which makes a PHP application even more flexible.

The inclusion of external files is performed using one of four different language constructs:

- `include`, which reads an external file and causes it to be interpreted. If the interpreter cannot find the file, it causes a warning to be produced and does *not* stop the execution of the script.

- `require`, which differs from `include` in the way it handles failure. If the file to be included cannot be found, `require` causes an error and stops the script's execution.

- `require_once` and `include_once`, which work in a similar way to `require` and `include`, with one notable difference: No matter how many times you include a particular file, `require_once` and `include_once` will only read it and cause it to be interpreted once.

The convenience of `require_once` and `include_once` is quite obvious because you don't have to worry about a particular file being included more than once in any given script—which would normally cause problems because everything that is part of the file would be interpreted more than once. However, generally speaking, situations in which a single file is included more than once are often an indicator that something is not right in the layout of your application. Using `require_once` or `include_once` will deprive you of an important debugging aid because you won't see any errors and, possibly, miss a problem of larger magnitude that is not immediately obvious. Still, in some cases there is no way around including a file more than once; therefore, these two constructs come in very handy.

Let's try an example. We'll start with a file that we will call `includefile.php`:

```php
<?php

echo 'You have included a file';

?>
```

Next, we'll move on to `mainfile.php`:

```php
<?php

include 'includefile.php';

echo 'I should have included a file.';

?>
```

If you make sure to put both files in the same directory and execute `mainfile.php`, you will notice that `includefile.php` is included and executed, causing the text `You have included a file` to be printed out.

Note that if the two files are not in the same folder, PHP will look for `includefile.php` in the *include path*. The include path is determined in part by the environment in which your script is running and by the php.ini settings that belong to your particular installation.

Manipulating Data

The manipulation of data is at the core of every language—and PHP is no exception. In fact, handling information of many different types is very often one of the primary tasks that a script must perform; it usually culminates with the output of some or all the data to a device—be it a file, the screen, or the Internet.

When dealing with data, it is often very important to know what *type* of data is being handled. If your application needs to know the number of times that a patient has visited the hospital, you want to make sure that the information provided by the user is, indeed, a number, and an integer number at that because it would be difficult for anybody to visit the hospital 3.5 times. Similarly, if you're asking for a person's name, you will, at the very least, ensure that you are not being provided with a number, and so on.

Like most modern languages, PHP supports a variety of data types and is capable of operating them in several different ways.

Numeric Values

PHP supports two numeric data types: integer and real (or floating-point). Both types correspond to the classic mathematical definition of the types—with the exception that real numbers are stored using a mechanism that makes it impossible to represent certain numbers, and with a somewhat limited precision so that, for example, 2 divided by 3 is represented as 0.66666666666667.

Numeric values in base 10 are represented only by digits and (optionally) a dot to separate units from fractional values. The interpreter does not need commas to group the integer portion of the value in thousands, nor does it understand it, producing an error if you use a format such as 123,456. Similarly, the European representation (comma to separate the fractional part of the value from the integer one) is not supported.

As part of your scripts, you can also enter a value in hexadecimal (base 16) representation—provided that it is prefixed by 0x, and that it is an integer. Both uppercase and lowercase hexadecimal digits are recognized by the interpreter, although traditionally only lowercase ones are actually used.

Finally, you can represent an integer value in octal (base 8) notation by prefixing it with a single zero and using only digits between 0 and 7. Thus, the value 0123 is *not* the same as 123. The interpreter will parse 0123 as an octal value, which actually corresponds to 83 in decimal representation (or 0x53 in hexadecimal).

String Values

Although we often think of strings as pieces of text, a string is best defined as a collection of bytes placed in a specific order. Thus, a string *could* contain text—say, for example, a user's first and last name—but it could also contain arbitrary binary data, such as the contents of a JPEG image of a MIDI file.

String values can be declared using one of three methods. The simplest one consists of enclosing your string in single quotes:

```
'This is a simple string'
```

The information between the quotes will be parsed by the interpreter and stored without any modification in the string. Naturally, you can include single quotation marks in your string by "escaping" them with a backslash:

```
'He said: \'This is a simple string\''
```

And this also means that, if you want to include a backslash, you will have to escape it as well:

```
'The file is in the c:\\test directory'
```

Another mechanism used to declare a string uses double quotation marks. This approach provides a bit more flexibility than the previous one, as you can now include a number of special characters through specific *escape sequences*:

- \n—A line feed
- \r—A carriage return
- \t—A horizontal tab
- \\—A backslash
- \"—A double quote
- \nnn—A character corresponding to the octal value of nnn (with each digit being between 0 and 7)
- \xnn—A character corresponding to the hexadecimal value of nn

Double-quote strings can also contain carriage returns. For example, the following strings are equivalent:

```
"This\nis a string"
"This
is a string"
```

The final method that you can use to declare a string is through the *heredoc* syntax:

```
<<<ENDOFTEXT
My text goes here.
More text can go on another line.
You can even use escape sequences: \t
ENDOFTEXT;
```

As you can see, the `<<<` heredoc tag is followed by an arbitrary string of text (which we'll call the *marker*) on a single line. The interpreter will parse the contents of the file as a string until the marker is found, on its own, at the beginning of a line, followed by a semicolon. Heredoc strings can come in handy when you want to embed large amounts of text in your scripts—although you can sometimes achieve a similar goal by simply switching in and out of PHP mode.

Boolean Values

A Boolean value can only be `True` or `False`. This type of value is generally used in Boolean expressions to change the flow of a script's execution based on certain conditions.

Note that, although PHP defines `True` and `False` as two valid values when printed, Boolean values are always an empty string (if false) or the number 1 (if true).

Arrays

Arrays are an *aggregate* value—that is, they represent a collection of other values. In PHP, arrays can contain an arbitrary number of elements of heterogeneous type (including other arrays). Each element is assigned a *key*—another scalar value used to identify the element within the array. You'll find this particular data type discussed in greater detail in Chapter 4, "Arrays."

Objects

Objects are self-contained collections of code and data. They are at the core of object-oriented programming and can provide a very valuable tool for creating solid, enterprise-level applications. They are described in Chapter 2, "Object-Oriented PHP."

The NULL Data Type

It is sometimes important to indicate that a datum has "no value". Computer languages need a special value for this purpose because even zero or an empty string imply that a value and a type have been assigned to a datum.

The NULL value, thus, is used to express the absence of *any* type of value.

Resources

A resource is a special type of value that indicates a reference to a resource that is external to your script and, therefore, not directly accessible from it.

For example, when you open a file so that you can add contents to it, the underlying code actually uses the operating system's functionality to create a file descriptor that can later be used for manipulating the file. This description can only be accessed by the functionality that is built into the interpreter and is, therefore, embedded in a resource value for your script to pass when taking advantage of the proper functionality.

Identifiers, Constants, and Variables

One of the most important aspects of any language is the capability to distinguish between its various components. To ensure that the interpreter is capable of recognizing each token of information passed to it properly, rules must be established for the purpose of being capable to tell each portion apart from the others.

In PHP, the individual tokens are separated from each other through "whitespace" characters, such as the space, tab, and newline character. Outside of strings, these characters have no semantic meaning—therefore, you can separate tokens with an arbitrary number of them. With one notable exception that we'll see in the next section, all tokens are not case sensitive—that is, `echo` is equivalent to `Echo`, or even `eCHo`.

Identifiers, which, as their name implies, are used as a label to identify data elements or groups of commands, must be named as follows:

- The first character can either be a letter or an underscore.
- Characters following the second can be an arbitrary combination of letters, digits, and underscores.

Thus, for example, the following are all valid identifiers:

- `__anidentifier`
- `yet_another_identifier___`
- `_3_stepsToSuccess`

Variables

As you can imagine, a language wouldn't be very useful if all it could deal with were immediate values: Using it would be a bit like buying a car with no doors or windows—sure, it can run fast, but to what purpose?

Similar to almost every computer language, PHP provides a facility known as a "variable" capable of containing data. PHP variables can contain one value at a time (although that value could, for example, be an array, which itself is a container for an arbitrary number of other values).

Variables are identifiers preceded by a dollar sign ($). Therefore, they must respect all the rules that determine how an identifier can be named. Additionally, variable names are case sensitive, so $myvar *is* different from $MyVar.

Unlike other languages, PHP does not require that the variables used by a script be declared before they can be used. The interpreter will create variables as they are used throughout the script.

Although this translates in a high degree of flexibility and generally nimbler scripts, it can also cause plenty of frustration and security issues. A simple spelling mistake, for example, could turn a reference to $myvar to, say, $mvvar, thus causing your script to reference a variable that doesn't exist. Similarly, if the installation of PHP that you are running has register_globals set to true, a malicious user will be able to set variables in your script to arbitrary values unless you take the proper precautions—more about that later in this chapter.

Variable Substitution in Strings

Both the double-quote and heredoc syntaxes support the ability to embed the value of a variable directly in a string:

```
"The value of \$a is $a"
```

In the preceding string, the second instance of $a will actually be replaced by the value of the $a variable, whereas the first instance will not because the dollar sign is escaped by a backslash.

For those cases in which this simple syntax won't work, such as when there is no whitespace between the name of the variable whose value you want to extract and the remainder of the string, you can forcefully isolate the data to be replaced by using braces:

```
<?

$thousands = 100;

echo "There are {$thousands}000 values";

?>
```

Statements

A statement corresponds to one command that the interpreter must execute. This could be an expression, a call to another block of code, or one of several constructs that PHP defines. For example, the echo construct causes the value of an expression to be sent to the script's output device.

Statements always end in a semicolon—if they don't, the system will output a parsing error.

Constants

As their name implies, constants are data holders whose type and value doesn't change.

A constant is create by using the `define()` construct. Here's an example:

```php
<?php

define ("SOME_CONSTANT", 28);

echo SOME_CONSTANT;

?>
```

As you can see, `define()` takes two parameters; the first, a string, indicates the name of the constant, whereas the second indicates its value. After you have defined a constant, you can use it directly from your code, as we have done here. This means that although, in theory, you can define a constant with an arbitrary name, you will only be able to use it if that name follows the identifier naming rules that we discussed in the previous sections.

Operators

Variables, constants, and data types are not very useful if you can't combine and manipulate them in a variety of ways. In PHP, one of these ways is through *operators*.

PHP recognizes several classes of operators, depending on what purpose they are used for.

The Assignment Operator

The assignment operator = is used to assign a value to a variable:

```php
$a = 10;
$c = "Greetings Professor Faulken";
$test = false;
```

It's very important to understand that, by default, variables are assigned *by value*. This means that the following

```php
$a = $b
```

Assigns the *value* of $b to $a. If you change $b after the assignment has taken place, $a will remain the same. This might not always be what you actually want to happen—you might need to link $a and $b so that a change to the latter is also reflected in the latter. You can do so by assigning to $a *a reference* to $b:

```php
$a = &$b
```

Any change to $b will now also be reflected in $a.

Arithmetic Operators

Perhaps the class of operators that most newcomers to PHP most readily identify with is the one that includes arithmetic operations. These are all part of binary operations (meaning that they always include two operators):

- Addition (+)
- Subtraction (-)
- Multiplication (*)
- Division (/)
- Modulus (%)

Operations are written using the infix notation that we are all used to. For example,

```
5 + 4
2 * $a
```

Keep in mind that the modulus operation works a bit different from the typical mathematical operation because it returns a signed value rather than an absolute one.

PHP also borrows four special incrementing/decrementing operators from the C language:

- The prefix incrementing operator ++ increments the value of the variable that succeeds it, and then returns its new value. For example, ++$a
- The postfix incrementing operator ++ returns the value of the variable that precedes it, and then increments its value. For example, $a++
- The prefix decrementing operator – decrements the value of the variable that succeeds it, and then returns its new value. For example, –$a
- The postfix decrementing operator – returns the value of the variable that precedes it, and then decrements its value. For example, $a–

The difference between the prefix and postfix version of the operators is sometimes difficult to grasp, but generally speaking is quite simple: The prefix version changes the value of the variable first, and then returns its value. This means that if the value of $a is 1, ++$a will first increment $a by one, and then return its value (which will be 2). Conversely, the postfix version returns the value first and then modifies it—so, if $a is 1, $a++ will first return 1 and then increment $a to 2.

Unary incrementing and decrementing operations can be extremely helpful because they enable for the modification of a variable in an atomic way and can easily be combined with other operations. However, this doesn't mean that they should be abused, as they can make the code more difficult to read.

Bitwise Operators

This class of operators manipulates the value of variables at the bit level:

- The bitwise AND (&)operation causes the value of a bit to be set if it is set in both the left and right operands. For example, `1 & 1 = 1`, whereas `1 & 2 = 0`.

- The bitwise OR (|) operation causes the value of a bit to be set if it is set in either the left or right operands. For example, `1 | 1 = 1` and `1 | 2 = 3`.

- The bitwise XOR (^) operation causes the value of a bit to be set if it is set in either the left or right operands, but not in both. For example, `1 ^ 1 = 0, 1 ^ 0 = 1`.

- The bitwise NOT (~)operation causes the bits in its operand to be reversed—that is, set if they are not and unset otherwise. Keep in mind that if you're dealing with an integer number, *all* the bits of that integer number will be reversed providing a value that you might not expect. For example, on a 32-bit IBM platform, where each integer is represented by a single 32-bit value, `~0 = -1`, because the integer is signed.

- The bitwise left-shift (<<) and right-shift (>>) operators actually shift the bits of the left operands left or right by the number of positions specified by the right operand. For example, `4 >> 1 = 2`, whereas `2 << 1 = 4`. On integer values, shifting bits to the left by n positions corresponds to multiplying the left operand by 2^n, whereas shifting them right by n position corresponds to dividing the left operand by 2^n.

Remember that bitwise operations can only be performed on integer values. If you use a value of a different type, PHP will convert it for you as appropriate or output an error if it can't.

Error-control Operators

PHP is normally very vocal when it finds something wrong with the code it's interpreting and executing, outputting verbose and helpful error messages to mark the occasion. Sometimes, however, it's practical to ensure that no error be reported, even if an error condition occurs.

This can be accomplished by using the error-suppression operator @ in front of the operation you want to perform. For example, the following would normally print an error because the result of a division by zero is infinity—a number that cannot be represented by any of the PHP data types. With the @ operator, however, we can prevent the error from being printed out (but *not* from occurring):

```php
<?php

@$a = 1 / 0;

?>
```

This operator can be very dangerous because it prevents PHP from notifying you that something has gone wrong. You should, therefore, use it only whenever you want to prevent errors from propagating to a default handler because you have a specialized code segment that you want to take care of the problem. Generally speaking, it's a bad idea to use this approach simply as a way to "silence" the PHP interpreter, as there are better ways to do so (for example, through error logging) without compromising its error reporting capabilities.

Note that not all types of errors can be caught and suppressed using the @ operator. Because PHP first parses your script into an intermediate language that makes execution faster and then executes it, it won't be capable of knowing that you have requested error suppression until the parsing phase is over and the execution phase begins. As a result, syntax errors that take place during the parsing phase will always result in an error being outputted, unless you have changed your php.ini settings in a way that prevents all errors from being outputted independently from your use of the @ operator.

String Operators

When it comes to manipulating strings, the only operator available is the concatenation operator, identified by a period (.). As you might imagine, it concatenates two strings into a third one, which is returned as the operation's result:

```php
<?php

$a = 'This is string ';
$b = $a . "is complete now.";

?>
```

Comparison Operators

Comparison operators are used to determine the relationship between two operands. The result of a comparison is always a Boolean value:

- The == operator determines if two values are equal. For example, 10 == 10
- The != operator determines if two values are different. For example, 10 != 11
- The < operator determines whether the left operand's value is less than the right operand's.
- The > operator determines whether the left operand's value is greater than the right operand's.
- The <= operator determines whether the left operand's value is less than or equal to the right operand's.
- The >= operator determines whether the left operand's value is greater than the right operand's.

To facilitate the operation of comparing two values, PHP will "automagically" perform a set of conversions to ensure that the two operands being compared will have the same type.

Thus, if you compare the number 10 with the string `"10"`, PHP will first convert the string to an integer number and then perform the comparison, whereas if you compare the integer 10 to the floating-point number 11.4, the former will be converted to a floating-point number first.

For the most part, this feature of PHP comes in very handy. However, in some cases it opens up a few potentially devastating pitfalls. For example, consider the string `"test"`. If you compare it against the number 0, PHP will first try to convert it to an integer number and, because `test` contains no digits, the result will be the value `0`. Now, it might not matter that the conversion took place, but if, for some reason, you really needed the comparison to be between two numbers, you will have a problem: `"11test"` compared against `11` will return `True`—and that might not exactly be what you were expecting!

Similarly, a `0` value can give you trouble if you're comparing a number against a Boolean value because `False` will be converted to 0 (and vice versa).

For those situations in which both the type and the value of a datum are both relevant to the comparison, PHP provides two "identity" operators:

- The `===` operator determines whether the value *and the type* of the two operands is the same.
- The `!==` operator determines whether either the value *or the type* of the two operands is different.

Thus, while `10 == "10"`, `10 !== "10"`.

Logical Operators

Logical operators are often used in conjunction with comparison operators to create complex decision mechanisms. They also return a Boolean result:

- The AND operator (indicated by the keyword `and` or by `&&`) returns `True` if both the left and right operands cannot be evaluated to `False`
- The OR operator (indicated by the keyword `or` or by `||`) returns `True` if either the left or right operand cannot be evaluated as `False`
- The XOR operator (indicated by the keyword `xor`) returns `True` if either the left or right operand can be evaluated as `True`, but not both.
- The unary NOT operator (indicated by `!`) returns `False` if the operand can be evaluated as `True`, and `True` otherwise.

Note that we used the term "can be evaluated as" rather than "is." This is because, even if one of the operands is not a Boolean value, the interpreter will try to convert it and use it as such. Thus, any number different from 0 is evaluated as `True`, as is every string that is not empty or is not `'0'`.

Typecasting

Even though PHP handles data types automatically most of the time, you can still force it to convert a particular datum to a specific type by using a typecasting operator. These are

- `(int)` to cast a value to its integer equivalent
- `(float)` to cast a value to its floating-point equivalent
- `(string)` to cast a value to its string equivalent
- `(array)` to force the conversion of the operand to an array if it is not one already
- `(object)` to force the conversion of the operand to an object if it is not one already

Keep in mind that some of these conversions fall prey to the same pitfalls that we discussed earlier for automatic conversions performed during comparisons.

Combined Assignment Operators

A particular class of operators combines the assignment of a value with another operation. For example, `+=` causes the left-hand operator to be added to the right-hand operator, and the result of the addition stored back in to the left-hand operator (which must, therefore, be a variable). For example,

```php
<?php

$a = 1;

$a += 5;

?>
```

At the end of the previous script's execution, `$a` will have a value of 6. All the binary arithmetic and bitwise operators can be part of one of these combined assignment operations.

Combining Operations: Operator Precedence and Associativity

Operator precedence determines in what order multiple combined operations that are part of the same expression are executed. For example, one of the basic rules of arithmetic is that multiplications and divisions are executed before additions and subtractions. With a large number of types of operations available, things get a bit more complicated, but are by no means complex.

When two operations having the same precedence must be performed one after the other, the concept of *associativity* comes in to play. A left-associative operation is executed from left to right. So, for example, `3 + 5 + 4 = (3 + 5) + 4`. A right-associative operation, on the other hand, is executed from right to left: $a += $b += 10 is equivalent to $a += ($b += 10). There are also some non-associative operations, such as comparisons. If two non-associative operations are on the same level of an expression, an error is produced. (If you think about it, an expression such as $a <= $b >= $c makes no sense in the context of a PHP script because the concept of "between" is not defined in the language. You would, in fact, have to rewrite that as ($a <= $b) && ($b >= $c).) Table 1.1 shows a list of operator precedences and associativity. Note that some of the operators will be introduced in Chapters 2 and 4.

Table 1.1 **Operator Precedence**

Associativity	Operator
right	[
right	! ~ ++ − (int) (float) (string) (array) (object) @
left	* / %
left	<< >>
non-associative	< <= > >=
non-associative	== != === !==
left	&
left	^
left	|
left	&&
left	||
left	? :
right	= += -= *= /= .= %= &= |= ^= <<= >>=
right	print
left	and
left	xor
left	or
left	,

As you have probably noticed, the logical operators && and || have a different precedence than and and or. This is an important bit of information that you should keep in mind while reading through PHP code.

Operator precedence can be overridden by using parentheses. For example,

```
10 * 5 + 2 = 52
10 & (5 + 2) = 70
```

Parentheses can be nested to an arbitrary number of levels—but, of course, the number of parentheses in an expression must be balanced.

Conditional Structures

It is often necessary, at some point, to change the execution of a script based on one or more conditions. PHP offers a set of structures that can be used to control the flow of execution as needed.

The simplest such structure is the `if-then-else` statement:

```
if (condition1)
    code-block-1
[else
    code-block-2...]
```

The series of commands `code-block-1` is executed if `condition1` can be evaluated to the Boolean value `True`, whereas `code-block-2` is executed if `condition1` can be evaluated to `False`. For example,

```php
<?php

$a = 10;

if ($a < 100)
    echo 'Less than 100';
else
    echo 'More than 100';

?>
```

In this case, the value of `$a` is obviously less than one hundred and, therefore, the first block of code will be executed, outputting `Less than 100`.

Clearly, if you could only include one instruction in every block of code, PHP would be extremely inefficient. Luckily, multiple instructions can be enclosed within braces:

```php
<?php

$a = 10;

if ($a < 100)
{
    echo 'Less than 100';
    echo "\nNow I can output more than one line!";
}
else
    echo 'More than 100';

?>
```

`if-then-else` statements can be nested to an arbitrary level. PHP even supports a special keyword, `elseif`, that makes this process easier:

```php
<?php

$a = 75;

if ($a > 100)
{
    echo 'More than 100';
    echo "Now I can output more than one line!";
}
elseif ($a > 50)
    echo 'More than 50';
else
    echo "I don't know what it is";

?>
```

In this case, the first condition (`$a > 100`) will not be satisfied. The execution point
will then move on to the second condition, (`$a > 50`), which *will* be satisfied, causing
the interpreter to output `More than 50`.

Alternative `if-then-else` Syntax

As an alternative to the `if-then-else` syntax described in the previous section, which is
what you will see in most modern PHP programs, PHP supports a different syntax in
which code blocks start with a semicolon and end with the keyword `endif`:

```php
<?php

$a = 10;

if ($a < 100):
    echo 'Less than 100';
    echo "Now I can output more than one line!";
elseif ($a < 50):
    echo 'Less than fifty';
else:
    echo "I don't know what it is";
endif

?>
```

Short-form `if-then-else`

A simple `if-then-else` statement can actually be written using a ternary operator (and,
therefore, inserted directly into a more complex operation):

```
<?

$n = 15;

$a = ($n % 2 ? 'odd number' : 'even number');

echo $a;

?>
```

As you can see, the ternary operator's syntax is

`(condition ? value_if_true : value_if_false)`

In the specific case here, the `value_if_true` is returned by the expression if `condition` evaluates to `True`; otherwise, `value_if_false` is returned instead.

The `case` Statement

A complex `if-then-else` statement, composed of an arbitrary number of conditions all based on the same expression being compared to a number of immediate values, can actually be replaced by a `case` statement as follows:

```
<?php

$a = 10;

switch ($a)
{
    case    '1':

        echo '1';
        break;

    case    '5':

        echo 'Five';
        break;

    case    'Ten':

        echo 'String 10';
        break;

    case    10:

        echo '10';
        break;
```

```
     default:

          echo 'I don\'t know what to do';
          break;
}
?>
```

When the interpreter encounters the `switch` keyword, it evaluates the expression that follows it and then compares the resulting value with each of the individual `case` conditions. If a match is found, the code is executed until the keyword `break` or the end of the switch code block is found, whichever comes first. If no match is found and the `default` code block is present, its contents are executed.

Note that the presence of the `break` statement is essential—if it is not present, the interpreter will continue to execute code in to the next `case` or `default` code block, which often (but not always) isn't what you want to happen. You can actually turn this behavior to your advantage to simulate a logical or operation; for example, this code

```
<?php

if ($a == 1 || $a == 2)
{
    echo 'test one';
}
else
{
    echo 'test two';
}

?>
```

Could be rewritten as follows:

```
<?php

switch ($a)
{
    case    1:
    case    2:

        echo 'test one';
        break;

    default:

        echo 'test two';
        break;
}

?>
```

Once inside the `switch` statement, a value of 1 or 2 will cause the same actions to take place.

Iteration and Loops

Scripts are often used to perform repetitive tasks. This means that it is sometimes necessary to cause a script to execute the same instructions for a number of times that might—or might not—be known ahead of time. PHP provides a number of control structures that can be used for this purpose.

The `while` Structure

A `while` statement executes a code block until a condition is set:

```php
<?php

$a = 10;

while ($a < 100)
{
    $a++;
}

?>
```

Clearly, you can use a condition that can never be satisfied—in which case, you'll end up with an *infinite loop*. Infinite loops are usually not a good thing, but, because PHP provides the proper mechanism for interrupting the loop at any point, they can also be useful. Consider the following:

```php
<?php

$a = 10;
$b = 50;

while (true)
{
    $a++;

    if ($a > 100)
    {
        $b++;
        if ($b > 50)
        {
            break;
        }
    }
}

?>
```

In this script, the (true) condition is always satisfied and, therefore, the interpreter will be more than happy to go on repeating the code block forever. However, inside the code block itself, we perform two if-then checks, and the second one is dependent on the first so that the $b > 50 will only be evaluated after $a > 100, and, if both are true, the break statement will cause the execution point to exit from the loop into the preceding scope. Naturally, we could have written this loop just by using the condition ($a <= 100 && $b <= 50) in the while loop, but it would have been less efficient because we'd have to perform the check twice. (Remember, $b doesn't increment unless $a is greater than 100.) If the second condition were a complex expression, our script's performance might have suffered.

The do-while Structure

The big problem with the while() structure is that, if the condition never evaluates to True, the statements inside the code block are never executed.

In some cases, it might be preferable that the code be executed at least once, and then the condition evaluated to determine whether it will be necessary to execute it again. This can be achieved in one of two ways: either by copying the code outside of the while loop into a separate code block, which is inefficient and makes your scripts more difficult to maintain, or by using a do-while loop:

```php
<?php

$a = 10;

do
{
    $a++;
}
while ($a < 10);

?>
```

In this simple script, $a will be incremented by one once—even if the condition in the do-while statement will never be true.

The for Loop

When you know exactly how many times a particular set of instructions must be repeated, using while and do-while loops is a bit inconvenient. For this purpose, for loops are also part of the arsenal at the disposal of the PHP programmer:

```php
<?php

for ($i = 10; $i < 100; $i++)
{
```

```
        echo $i;
}

?>
```

As you can see, the declaration of a `for` loop is broken in to three parts: The first is used to perform any initialization operations needed and is executed only once *before* the loop begins. The second represents the condition that must be satisfied for the loop to continue. Finally, the third contains a set of instructions that are executed once at the end of every iteration of the loop before the condition is tested.

A `for` loop could, in principle, be rewritten as a `while` loop. For example, the previous simple script can be rewritten as follows:

```
<?php

$i = 10;

while ($i < 100)
{
    echo $i;
    $i++;
}

?>
```

As you can see, however, the `for` loop is much more elegant and compact.

Note that you can actually include more than one operation in the initialization and end-of-loop expressions of the `for` loop declaration by separating them with a comma:

```
<?php

for ($i = 1, $c = 2; $i < 10; $i++, $c += 2)
{
    echo $i;
    echo $c;
}

?>
```

Naturally, you can also create a `for` loop that is infinite—in a number of ways, in fact. You could omit the second expression from the declaration, which would cause the interpreter to always evaluate the condition to true. You could omit the third expression and never perform any actions in the code block associated with the loop that will cause the condition in the second expression to be evaluated as true. You can even omit all three expressions using the form `for(;;)` and end up with the equivalent of `while(true)`.

Continuing a Loop

You have already seen how the `break` statement can be used to exit from a loop. What if, however, you simply want to skip until the end of the code block associated with the loop and move on to the next iteration?

In that case, you can use the `continue` statement:

```php
<?php

for ($i = 1, $c = 2; $i < 10; $i++, $c += 2)
{
    if ($c < 10)
        continue;

    echo 'I\'ve reached 10!';
}

?>
```

If you nest more than one loop, you can actually even specify the number of loops that you want to skip and move on from:

```php
<?php

for ($i = 1, $c = 2; $i < 10; $i++, $c += 2)
{
    $b = 0;

    while ($b < 199) {
        if ($c < 10)
            continue 2;

        echo 'I\'ve reached 10!';
    }
}

?>
```

In this case, when the execution reaches the inner `while` loop, if `$c` is less than `10`, the `continue 2` statement will cause the interpreter to skip back two loops and start over with the next iteration of the `for` loop.

Functions and Constructs

The code that we have looked at up to this point works using a very simple top-down execution style: The interpreter simply starts at the beginning and works its way to the end in a linear fashion. In the real world, this simple approach is rarely practical; for example, you might want to perform a certain operation more than once in different portions of your code. To do so, PHP supports a facility known as a *function*.

Functions must be declared using the following syntax:

```
function function_name ([param1[, paramn]])
```

As you can see, each function is assigned a name and can receive one or more parameters. The parameters exist as variables throughout the execution of the entire function.

Let's look at an example:

```php
<?php

function calc_weeks ($years)
{
    return $years * 52;
}

$my_years = 28;
echo calc_weeks ($my_years);

?>
```

The $years variable is created whenever the calc_weeks function is called and initialized with the value passed to it. The return statement is used to return a value from the function, which then becomes available to the calling script. You can also use return to exit from the function at any given time.

Normally, parameters are passed by value—this means that, in the previous example, a copy of the $my_years variable is placed in the $years variable when the function begins, and any changes to the latter are not reflected in the former. It is, however, possible to force passing a parameter *by reference* so that any changes performed within the function to it will be reflected on the outside as well:

```php
<?php

function calc_weeks (&$years)
{
    $my_years += 10;
    return $my_years * 52;
}

$my_years = 28;
echo calc_weeks ($my_years);

?>
```

You can also assign a *default value* to any of the parameters of a function when declaring it. This way, if the caller does not provide a value for the parameter, the default one will be used instead:

```php
<?php

function calc_weeks ($my_years = 10)
{

    return $my_years * 52;
}

echo calc_weeks ();

?>
```

In this case, because no value has been passed for $my_years, the default of 10 will be used by the interpreter. Note that you can't assign a default value to a parameter passed by reference.

Functions and Variable Scope

It's important to note that there is no relationship between the name of a variable declared inside a function and any corresponding variables declared outside of it. In PHP, variable scope works differently from most other languages so that what resides in the global scope is not automatically available in a function's scope. Let's look at an example:

```php
<?php

function calc_weeks ()
{
    $years += 10;
    return $years * 52;
}

$years = 28;
echo calc_weeks ();

?>
```

In this particular case, the script assumes that the $years variable, which is part of the global scope, will be automatically included in the scope of calc_weeks(). However, this does not take place, so $years has a value of Null inside the function, resulting in a return value of 0.

If you want to import global variables inside a function's scope, you can do so by using the global statement:

```php
<?php

function calc_weeks ()
{
    global $years;
```

```
    $years += 10;
    return $years * 52;
}

$years = 28;
echo calc_weeks ();

?>
```

The $years variable is now available to the function, where it can be used and modified. Note that by importing the variable inside the function's scope, any changes made to it will be reflected in the global scope as well—in other words, you'll be accessing the variable itself, and not an ad hoc copy as you would with a parameter passed by value.

Functions with Variable Parameters

It's sometimes impossible to know how many parameters are needed for a function. In this case, you can create a function that accepts a variable number of arguments using a number of functions that PHP makes available for you:

- func_num_args() returns the number of parameters passed to a function.
- func_get_arg($arg_num) returns a particular parameter, given its position in the parameter list.
- func_get_args() returns an array containing all the parameters in the parameter list.

As an example, let's write a function that calculates the arithmetic average of all the parameters passed to it:

```
<?php

function calc_avg()
{
    $args =  func_num_args();

    if ($args == 0)
        return 0;

    $sum = 0;

    for ($i = 0; $i < $args; $i++)
        $sum += func_get_arg($i);

    return $sum / $args;
}

echo calc_avg (19, 23, 44, 1231, 2132, 11);

?>
```

As you can see, we start by determining the number of arguments and exiting immediately if there are none. We need to do so because otherwise the last instruction would cause a division-by-zero error. Next, we create a `for` loop that simply cycles through each parameter in sequence, adding its value to the sum. Finally, we calculate and return the average value by dividing the sum by the number of parameters. Note how we stored the value of the parameter count in the `$args` variable—we did so in order to make the script a bit more efficient because otherwise we would have had to perform a call to `func_get_args()` for every cycle of the `for` loop. That would have been rather wasteful because a function call is quite expensive in terms of performance and the number of parameters passed to the function does not change during its execution.

Variable Variables and Variable Functions

PHP supports two very useful features known as "variable variables" and "variable functions."

The former allows you use the value of a variable as the name of a variable. Sound confusing? Look at this example:

```
<?

$a = 100;
$b = 'a';

echo $$b;

?>
```

When this script is executed and the interpreter encounters the $$b expression, it first determines the value of $b, which is the string a. It then reevaluates the expression with a substituted for $b as $a, thus returning the value of the $a variable.

Similarly, you can use a variable's value as the name of a function:

```
<?

function odd_number ($x)
{
    echo "$x is odd";
}

function even_number ($x)
{
    echo "$x is even";
}

$n = 15;

$a = ($n % 2 ? 'odd_number' : 'even_number');
```

```
$a($n);

?>
```

At the end of the script, $a will contain either odd_number or even_number. The expression $a($n) will then be evaluated as a call to either odd_number() or even_number().

Variable variables and variable functions can be extremely valuable and convenient. However, they tend to make your code obscure because the only way to really tell what happens during the script's execution is to execute it—you can't determine whether what you have written is correct by simply looking at it. As a result, you should only really use variable variables and functions when their usefulness outweighs the potential problems that they can introduce.

Exam Prep Questions

1. What will the following script output?

```
<?php

$x = 3 - 5 % 3;

echo $x;

?>
```

   A. 2
   B. 1
   C. Null
   D. True
   E. 3

   Answer **B** is correct. Because of operator precedence, the modulus operation is performed first, yielding a result of 2 (the remainder of the division of 5 by 2). Then, the result of this operation is subtracted from the integer 3.

2. Which data type will the $a variable have at the end of the following script?

```
<?php

$a = "1";

echo $x;

?>
```

A. (int) 1

B. (string) "1"

C. (bool) True

D. (float) 1.0

E. (float) 1

Answer **B** is correct. When a numeric string is assigned to a variable, it remains a string, and it is not converted until needed because of an operation that requires so.

3. What will the following script output?

```php
<?php

$a = 1;

$a = $a- + 1;

echo $a;

?>
```

A. 2

B. 1

C. 3

D. 0

E. Null

Answer **A** is correct. The expression $a- will be evaluated after the expression $a = $a + 1 but *before* the assignment. Therefore, by the time $a + 1 is assigned to $a, the increment will simply be lost.

2

Object-Oriented PHP

DESPITE BEING A RELATIVELY RECENT—and often maligned—addition to the computer programming world, object-oriented programming (OOP) has rapidly taken hold as the programming methodology of choice for the enterprise.

The basic concept behind OOP is *encapsulation*—the grouping of data and code elements that share common traits inside a container known as a *class*. Classes can be organized hierarchically so that any given one can *inherit* some or all the characteristics of another one. This way, new code can build on old code, making for more stable and reliable code (at least, in theory).

Because it was added by the designers almost as an afterthought, the implementation of OOP in PHP 4 differs from the traditional implementations provided by most other languages in that it does not follow the traditional tenets of object orientation and is, therefore, fraught with peril for the programmer who approaches it coming from a more traditional platform.

Terms You'll Need to Understand

- Namespace
- Class
- Object
- Method
- Property
- Class member
- Instantiation
- Constructor
- Inheritance
- Magic function

Techniques You'll Need to Master

- OOP fundamentals
- Writing classes
- Instantiating objects
- Accessing class members
- Creating derivate classes
- Serializing and unserializing objects

Getting Started

As we mentioned previously, the basic element of OOP is the *class*. A class contains the definition of data elements (or *properties*) and functions (or *methods*) that share some common trait and can be encapsulated in a single structure.

In PHP, a class is declared using the `class` construct:

```php
<?php

class my_class
{
    var $my_var;

    function my_class ($var)
    {
        $this->my_var = $my_var;
    }
}

?>
```

As you can see here, the `class` keyword is followed by the name of the class, `my_class` in our case, and then by a code block where a number of properties and methods are defined.

Data properties are defined by using the `var` keyword followed by the name of the variable. You can even assign a value to the property by using the following syntax:

```php
var $my_var = 'a value';
```

Following property declarations, we define a method, which in this special case has the same name as the class. This designates it as the class' *constructor*—a special method that is automatically called by the interpreter whenever the class is instantiated.

You'll notice that, inside the constructor, the value of the `$var` parameter is assigned to the `$my_var` data property by using the syntax `$this->my_var = $var`. The `$this` variable is a reference to the current object that is only available from within the methods of a particular class. You can use it to access the various methods and properties of the class. Thus, $this means "the current instance of the class," whereas the -> indirection operator informs the interpreter that you're trying to access a property or method of the class. As you can imagine, methods are accessed as $this->method().

Instantiating a Class: Objects

You cannot use a class directly—it is, after all, nothing more than the declaration of a special kind of data type. What you must do is to actually *instantiate it* and create an *object*. This can be done by using the new operator, which has the highest possible precedence:

```php
<?php

class my_class
{
    var $my_var;

    function my_class ($var)
    {
        $this->my_var = $my_var;
    }
}

$obj = new my_class ("something");

echo $obj->my_var;

?>
```

The new operator causes a new instance of the my_class class to be created and assigned to $obj. Because my_class has a constructor, the object's instantiation automatically calls it, and we can pass parameters to it directly.

From this point on, properties and methods of the object can be accessed using a syntax similar to the one that we saw in the previous section except, of course, that $this doesn't exist outside the scope of the class itself, and instead we must use the name of the variable to which we assigned the object.

Classes as Namespaces

After a class is defined, its methods can be accessed in one of two ways: dynamically, by instatiating an object, or statically, by treating the class as a *namespace*. Essentially, namespaces are nothing more than containers of methods:

```php
<?php

class base_class
{
    var    $var1;

    function base_class ($value)
    {
        $this->var1 = $value;
    }

    function calc_pow ($base, $exp)
    {
        return pow ($base, $exp);
    }
}

echo base_class::calc_pow (3, 4);

?>
```

As you can see in the previous example, the : : operator can be used to statically address one of the methods of a class and execute it. Grouping a certain number of methods into a class and then using that class as a namespace can make it easier to avoid naming conflicts in your library, but, generally speaking, that's not reason enough by itself to justify the overhead caused by using classes.

Objects and References

The biggest problem working with objects is passing them around to function calls. This is because objects behave in exactly the same way as every other data type: By default, they are passed by value. Unlike most other values, however, you will almost always cause an object to be modified when you use it.

Let's take a look at an example:

```php
<?php

class my_class
{
    var $my_var;

    function my_class ($var)
    {
        global $obj_instance;
```

```
            $obj_instance = $this;
            $this->my_var = $var;
    }
}

$obj = new my_class ("something");

echo $obj->my_var;
echo $obj_instance->my_var;

?>
```

As you can see, the constructor here assigns the value of $this to the global variable $obj_instance. When the value of $obj_instance->my_var is printed out later in the script, however, the expected something doesn't show up—and the property actually has a value of NULL.

To understand why, you need to consider two things. First, when $this is assigned to $obj_instance, it is assigned by value, and this causes PHP to actually create a copy of the object so that when $var is assigned to $this->my_var, there no longer is any connection between the current object and what is stored in $obj_instance.

You might think that assigning $this by reference might make a difference:

```
<?php

class my_class
{
    var $my_var;

    function my_class ($var)
    {
        global $obj_instance;

        $obj_instance = &$this;
        $this->my_var = $var;
    }
}

$obj = new my_class ("something");

echo $obj->my_var;
echo $obj_instance->my_var;

?>
```

Unfortunately, it doesn't—as much as this might seem extremely odd, you'll find the following even stranger:

```php
<?php

class my_class
{
    var $my_var;

    function my_class ($var)
    {
        global $obj_instance;

        $obj_instance[] = &$this;
        $this->my_var = $var;
    }
}

$obj = new my_class ("something");

echo $obj->my_var;
echo $obj_instance[0]->my_var;

?>
```

Assigning a reference to $this to a scalar variable hasn't helped, but by making $obj_instance an array, the reference was properly passed. The main problem here is that the $this variable is really a special variable built ad hoc for the internal use of the class—and you really shouldn't rely on it being used for anything external at all.

Even though this solution seems to work, incidentally, it really didn't. Try this:

```php
<?php

class my_class
{
    var $my_var;

    function my_class ($var)
    {
        global $obj_instance;

        $obj_instance[] = &$this;
        $this->my_var = $var;
    }
}

$obj = new my_class ("something");

$obj->my_var = "nothing";
```

```php
echo $obj->my_var;
echo $obj_instance[0]->my_var;

?>
```

If `$obj_instance` had really become a reference to `$obj`, we would expect a change to the latter to be reflected also in the former. However, as you can see if you run the preceding script, after we have changed the value of `$obj->my_var` to nothing, `$obj_instance` still contains the old value.

How is this possible? Well, the problem is in the fact that `$obj` was created with a simple assignment. So what really happened is that new created a new instance of `my_class`, and a reference to that instance was assigned to `$obj_instance` by the constructor. When the instance was assigned to `$obj`, however, it was assigned *by value*— therefore, a copy was created, leading to the two variables holding two distinct copies of the same object. In order to obtain the effect we were looking for, we have to change the assignment so that it, too, is done by reference:

```php
<?php

class my_class
{
    var $my_var;

    function my_class ($var)
    {
        global $obj_instance;

        $obj_instance[] = &$this;
        $this->my_var = $var;
    }
}

$obj = &new my_class ("something");

$obj->my_var = "nothing";

echo $obj->my_var;
echo $obj_instance[0]->my_var;

?>
```

Now, at last, `$obj_instance` is a proper reference to `$obj`.

Generally speaking, this is the greatest difficulty that faces the user of objects in PHP. Because they are treated as normal scalar values, you must assign them by reference whenever you pass them along to a function or assign them to a variable.

Naturally, you can turn this quirk in PHP 4 to your advantage as well by using a by-value assignment whenever you want to make a copy of an object. Be careful, however, that even the copy operation might not be what you expect. For example, if your object includes one or more variables that contain resources, only the variables will be duplicated, not the resources themselves. This difference is subtle, but very important because the underlying resources will remain the same so that when they are altered by one object, the changes will be reflected in the copy as well.

Implementing Inheritance

Classes can gain each other's properties and methods through a process known as *inheritance*. In PHP, inheritance is implemented by "extending" a class:

```php
<?php

class base_class
{
    var     $var1;

    function base_class ($value)
    {
        $this->var1 = $value;
    }

    function calc_pow ($exp)
    {
        return pow ($this->var1, $exp);
    }
}

class new_class extends base_class
{
    var $var2;

    function new_class ($value)
    {
        $this->var2 = $value;
        $this->var1 = $value * 10;
    }
}

$obj = new new_class (10);

echo $obj->calc_pow (4);

?>
```

As you can see here, the extends keyword is used to add the methods and properties of the base class base_class to new_class, which defines new variables and a new constructor. The calc_pow function, which is defined in the base class, becomes immediately available to the new class and can be called as if it were one of its methods.

Note, however, that only the constructor for the new class is called—the old class' is completely ignored. This might not be always what you want—in which case, you can access each of the parent's methods statically through the parent built-in namespace that PHP defines for you inside your object:

```php
<?php

class base_class
{
    var     $var1;

    function base_class ($value)
    {
        $this->var1 = $value;
    }

    function calc_pow ($exp)
    {
        return pow ($this->var1, $exp);
    }
}

class new_class extends base_class
{
    var $var2;

    function new_class ($value)
    {
        $this->var2 = $value;

        parent::base_class ($value);
    }
}

$obj = new new_class (10);

echo $obj->calc_pow (4);

?>
```

In this example, the parent constructor is called by the new constructor as if it were a normal static function, although the former will have at its disposal all of its normal methods and properties.

The great advantage of inheritance is that it provides a simple mechanism for extending the capabilities of your code in a gradual way without having to rewrite loads of code every time.

Magic Functions: Serializing Objects

You might sometimes want objects to be passed along between different calls to your scripts—for example, from one page to the next. One way to do so is to use a process known as "serialization" in which the contents of the object are saved and then the object is re-created by reversing the process.

In PHP, this can be performed automatically by PHP by simply saving all the object's properties and then storing them back in the object when it is rebuilt. In some cases, however, this is not what you might want. For example, one of your properties could be a file resource—in which case, you would have to close the file when the object is serialized and then open it again when it is unserialized.

In these instances, PHP can't do the job for you, but you can implement two "magic" functions to do whatever you need on an ad hoc basis:

```php
<?php

class base_class
{
    var    $var1;
    var $var2;

    function base_class ($value)
    {
        $this->var1 = $value;
        $this->var2 = $value * 100;
    }

    function calc_pow ($exp)
    {
        return pow ($var1, $exp);
    }

    function __sleep()
    {
        // Return an array that contains
        // the name of all the variables to be saved

        return array ('var1');
    }

    function __wakeup()
    {
```

```
    // Reconstruct $var2

    $this->var2 = $this->var1 * 100;
  }
}

?>
```

As you can see, the `__sleep` function is called whenever an object is serialized. It returns an array that contains the names (minus the dollar sign) of all the data members that must be saved. In our case, `base_class::var2` is actually derived directly from the value of `base_class::var1`, so we don't want to save it. When the object is unserialized, the interpreter will call `__wakeup()` in which we take the opportunity to rebuild `$var2` with the appropriate value.

Exam Prep Questions

1. What will the following script output?

```php
<?php

class a
{
    var $c;

    function a ($pass)
    {
        $this->c = $pass;
    }

    function print_data()
    {
        echo $this->$c;
    }
}

$a = new a(10);
$a->print_data();

?>
```

    A. An error

    B. 10

    C. "10"

    D. Nothing

    E. A warning

Answer **D** is correct. There actually is a bug in the `print_data()` function—`$this->$c` is interpreted as a variable by PHP, and because the `$c` variable is not defined inside the function, no information will be available for printing. Note that if error reporting had been turned on, either through a `php.ini` setting or through an explicit call to `error_reporting()`, two warnings would have been outputted instead—but, unless the exam question tells you otherwise, you should assume that the normal PHP configuration is being used. And in that case, the interpreter is set not to report warnings.

2. When serializing and unserializing an object, which of the following precautions should you keep in mind? (Choose two)

   A. Always escape member properties that contain user input.

   B. If the object contains resource variables, use magic functions to restore the resources upon unserialization.

   C. Use the magic functions to only save what is necessary.

   D. Always use a transaction when saving the information to a database.

   E. If the object contains resource variables, it cannot be serialized without first destroying and releasing its resources.

   Answers **B** and **C** are correct. Whenever you design an object that is meant to be serialized or that can contain resource objects, you should implement the appropriate magic functions to ensure that it is serialized and unserialized properly—and using the smallest amount of information possible.

3. What will the following script output?

```php
<?php

error_reporting(E_ALL);

class a
{
    var $c;

    function a()
    {
        $this->c = 10;
    }
}

class b extends a
{
```

```
    function print_a()
    {
        echo $this->c;
    }
}

$b = new b;
$b->print_a();

?>
```

    A. Nothing

    B. An error because b does not have a constructor

    C. 10

    D. NULL

    E. False

Answer **C** is correct. Because the class b does not have a constructor, the constructor of its parent class is executed instead. This results in the value 10 being assigned to the $c member property.

3

PHP and the Web

Terms You'll Need to Understand

- Server-side
- Client-side
- Hypertext Transfer Protocol (HTTP)
- GET request
- POST request
- Superglobal array
- HTTP header
- Cookie
- Session
- Session identifier

Techniques You'll Need to Master

- Distinguishing between server-side and client-side
- Handling form data using superglobal arrays
- Working with cookies
- Persisting data in sessions

Server-side Versus Client-side

One of the keys to understanding PHP's role in the Web is to understand how the Web works at a fundamental level. This generally involves a basic understanding of HTTP, Hypertext Transfer Protocol. To examine the basic operation of the Web, consider a typical HTTP client, your Web browser. When you visit a URL such as http://example.org/, your browser sends an HTTP request to the web server at `example.org`. The simplest example of this request is as follows:

```
GET / HTTP/1.1
Host: example.org
```

The web server's responsibility is to respond to this request, preferably with the resource that is desired (the document root in this example). An example of a response is as follows:

```
HTTP/1.1 200 OK
Content-Type: text/html
Content-Length: 419

<html>
<head><title>Example Web Page</title></head>
<body>
<p>You have reached this web page by typing &quot;example.com&quot;,
&quot;example.net&quot;, or &quot;example.org&quot; into your web browser.</p>
<p>These domain names are reserved for use in documentation and are not
available for registration. See
<a href="http://www.rfc-editor.org/rfc/rfc2606.txt">RFC 2606</a>, Section
3.</p>
</body>
</html>
```

As you should notice, the majority of this response is the actual content, the HTML. When your browser receives this response, it will render the web page (see Figure 3.1). Once a page is rendered, you can disconnect your computer from the Internet, and this won't cause a problem until your browser needs to send another HTTP request.

Where does PHP fit into this process? PHP's role is best explained as an aid to the web server while it is generating the HTTP response. Thus, by the time the web server sends the response, PHP's job is done. Its output is included in the response. Because PHP's activity takes place on the server, it is an example of a server-side technology.

By contrast, any processing that takes place after the browser has received the response is referred to as client-side. JavaScript is a popular choice for client-side scripting. You're probably familiar with using JavaScript or at least seeing it when you view the source of a web page. This is a distinguishing characteristic. What you see when you view the source of a web page is the content of the HTTP request. This content can be generated on the server, so just as PHP can be used to generate HTML, it can also generate JavaScript.

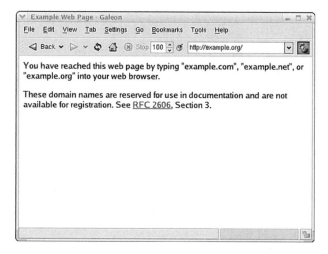

Figure 3.1   A browser renders a web page.

JavaScript executes on the client. Thus, interacting with PHP is much more difficult because it requires another HTTP request to be sent. After all, PHP's job is done, and the web server is quietly awaiting the next request. By the time JavaScript executes, there isn't even a connection between the Web client (your browser) and the web server anymore.

If you find yourself having trouble determining whether you can pass data from PHP to JavaScript or from JavaScript to PHP, it would be wise to review this section a few times. A clear understanding of the environment in which PHP operates, and the distinction between client-side and server-side technologies, is important.

HTML Forms

One task with which you should already be familiar is processing HTML forms. Forms provide a convenient way for users to send data to the server, and this makes the Web much more interactive. PHP makes processing these forms easy for developers; the form data is available in the $_GET and $_POST superglobal arrays, depending on the method used in the form (which in turn affects the request method used by the browser). In addition, $_REQUEST is a method-agnostic array that you can use to access form data (basically a merge of both $_GET and $_POST).

Superglobal arrays are available in every scope, which makes them convenient to use. For example, you might use them in a function without having to declare them as global, and there is no need to ever pass them to a function. They are always available.

For versions of PHP prior to 4.1.0, you must use a different set of arrays because $_GET, $_POST, and $_REQUEST are not available. Instead, you must use $_HTTP_GET_VARS and $_HTTP_POST_VARS (for $_GET and $_POST, respectively). There is no equivalent for $_REQUEST (where both arrays are merged), and these are also not superglobals, so you must use them similar to standard arrays.

To illustrate how form data is passed, consider the following form:

```
<form action="/process.php" method="post">
<input type="text" name="answer" />
<input type="submit" />
</form>
```

Figure 3.2 shows how this form appears in a Web browser.

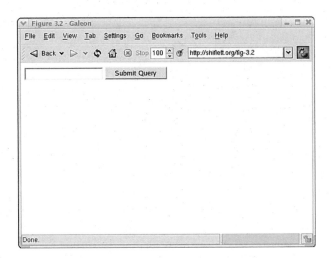

Figure 3.2   A browser renders an HTML form.

If a user enters C for the answer and submits the form, an HTTP request similar to the following is sent to the web server:

```
POST /process.php HTTP/1.1
Host: example.org
Content-Type: application/x-www-form-urlencoded
Content-Length: 8

answer=C
```

As a PHP developer, you can reference this value as $_POST['answer'] because the request method (indicated on the first line of the HTTP request) is POST.

By contrast, if the method of the form specifies the use of a GET request, the request is similar to the following:

```
GET /process.php?answer=C HTTP/1.1
Host: example.org
```

Rather than passing the form data as the content of the request, it is passed as the query string of the URL. In this situation, you can reference $_GET['answer'] to get the user's answer.

One important point about HTML forms is that the result of any form element is a single name/value pair in the request. This is true for hidden form elements, radio buttons, checkboxes, and all other types. For example, consider the following form:

```
<form action="/process.php" method="post">
<input type="hidden" name="answer" value="C" />
<input type="submit" />
</form>
```

Figure 3.3 shows how this form appears in a Web browser. Unlike the previous example, the user is only presented with the submit button. As long as the user uses this form to send the POST request, the value of $_POST['answer'] will always be C. The actual request sent by the browser is identical to the previous example, thus it is impossible to discern the type of HTML form used to generate a request by only observing the request.

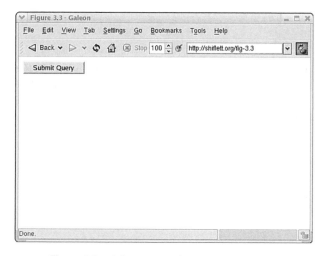

Figure 3.3 A browser renders an HTML form.

The behavior of some form elements can be confusing. Notably, elements such as check boxes and radio buttons, because of their Boolean nature, are only included in the request if selected. When selected, their value is determined by the value attribute given in the HTML markup. Thus, the corresponding variable in PHP might or might not be set, and you might want to use isset() on these types of elements to determine this.

There is also the special case in which multiple form elements are given the same name, such as in the following example:

```
<form action="/process.php" method="post">
<input type="text" name="answer" />
<input type="text" name="answer" />
<input type="submit" />
</form>
```

The browser will send a request similar to the following (assuming that the user answers c and A, respectively):

```
POST /process.php HTTP/1.1
Host: example.org
Content-Type: application/x-www-form-urlencoded
Content-Length: 8

answer=C&answer=A
```

If you reference $_POST['answer'], you will notice that its value is A. Where did the first answer go? As PHP processes the form for you and assigns variables within the superglobal arrays, values can be overwritten. If this is not the desired behavior, there is a simple naming convention you can use instead:

```
<form action="/process.php" method="post">
<input type="text" name="answer[]" />
<input type="text" name="answer[]" />
<input type="submit" />
</form>
```

By adding [] to the end of the form element name, you are asking PHP to create an array for this particular element. Assuming that the same answers as before (c and A, respectively) are entered before submitting the form, $_POST['answer'] is now an enumerated array, and the output of print_r($_POST['answer']) is as follows:

```
Array
(
    [0] => C
    [1] => A
)
```

So, you now have both values preserved conveniently in an array.

Cookies

What are cookies? When described as entities, which is how cookies are often referenced in conversation, you can be easily misled. Cookies are actually just an extension of the HTTP protocol. Specifically, there are two additional HTTP headers: Set-Cookie and Cookie. The operation of these cookies is best described by the following series of events:

1. Client sends an HTTP request to server.
2. Server sends an HTTP response with Set-Cookie: foo=bar to client.
3. Client sends an HTTP request with Cookie: foo=bar to server.
4. Server sends an HTTP response to client.

Thus, the typical scenario involves two complete HTTP transactions. In step 2, the server is asking the client to return a particular cookie in future requests. In step 3, if the user's preferences are set to allow cookies, and if the cookie is valid for this particular request, the browser requests the resource again but includes the cookie.

Hopefully this simple explanation already makes it clear why you cannot determine whether a user's preferences are set to allow cookies during the first request. When you set a cookie in your PHP code, whether by using `setcookie()` or `header()`, all you are doing is modifying the HTTP response to include a `Set-Cookie` header. You cannot, during the time that you are generating this response, determine how the browser will react. After all, the browser won't even receive the response (and the `Set-Cookie` header) until PHP has finished executing.

The `Set-Cookie` header, at a minimum, contains the name and value of the cookie. For example,

```
Set-Cookie: foo=bar
```

Other attributes can be included to modify when the cookie is to be sent in a subsequent request. These optional attributes are as follows:

- `domain`—Restricts requests for which the cookie is sent to those that are within the specified domain or in subdomains. The default is the domain of the current resource.

- `expires`—A date after which the cookie is no longer valid and should be deleted. The default is to persist the cookie in memory only, expiring it as soon as the browser ends.

- `path`—Only requests for resources within the specified path include the cookie. The default is no path restrictions.

- `secure`—An attribute with no value that indicates that the cookie should only be sent in requests sent over a secure connection, such as SSL.

An example of a `Set-Cookie` header with all optional attributes is as follows:

```
Set-Cookie: foo=bar; domain=example.org; expires=Mon, 26 Jul 2004 12:34:56 GMT;
➥ path=/; secure
```

The `Cookie` header included in subsequent requests contains only the name and value of the cookie:

```
Cookie: foo=bar
```

The attributes included in the `Set-Cookie` header are only used to determine whether the cookie should be included in the request at all. If included, only the name and value are given. In PHP, cookies sent in the request are made available in the `$_COOKIE` superglobal array (for PHP versions prior to 4.1.0, cookies are available in the `$_HTTP_COOKIE_VARS` array).

Sessions

One common use of cookies, and one of the main reasons behind their inception, is to maintain state. Stated differently, cookies allow you to associate separate HTTP transactions together by identifying a specific client.

If you set a cookie with a unique identifier, you can store information about the client on the server, and on the next request from that same client, you can use the cookie to identify the client and fetch the data that you stored. This technique is known as *session management*, and it relies on the ability to maintain state.

PHP makes all of this easy with its built-in sessions. To initiate PHP's sessions, simply include the following function call on any PHP page:

```
session_start();
```

If you are using the default `php.ini`, this function requires PHP to manipulate some HTTP headers, so you must call it prior to any output. After you have called this function, you can simply use the `$_SESSION` superglobal array to store and access session variables. (For PHP versions prior to 4.1.0, `$_HTTP_SESSION_VARS` must be used instead.) For example, the following code sets a session variable named `foo`:

```
$_SESSION['foo'] = 'bar';
```

PHP takes care of propagating the session identifier (the unique identifier used to distinguish each client from any other) in a cookie or on the URL, depending on your `php.ini` settings, and it also takes care of storing and retrieving the session data.

Quite a few directives in `php.ini` affect sessions. The most notable ones are as follows:

- `session.save_path`—This indicates the directory in which PHP will store session data.
- `session.use_cookies`—This is a Boolean that indicates whether PHP will use cookies to propagate the session identifier.
- `session.use_only_cookies`—This is a Boolean that indicates whether PHP will only check cookies for a session identifier (and not the URL).
- `session.name`—The name of the session (also used as the name of the session identifier).
- `session.auto_start`—This is a Boolean that indicates whether PHP should always enable session management, allowing you to avoid the call to `session_start()`.
- `session.cookie_lifetime, session.cookie_path, session.cookie_domain`—These correspond to the attributes used in the `Set-Cookie` header for the session identifier.

- `session.use_trans_sid`—This is a Boolean that indicates whether PHP should dynamically choose whether to propagate the session identifier via cookies or the URL, depending on the user's preferences. If cookies are enabled, PHP will use a cookie; otherwise, it will use the URL. On the first page, PHP will use both methods since it cannot yet determine whether the user's preferences allow cookies (recall the previous discussion on cookies).

By default, PHP stores session data on the filesystem. If you want to modify this behavior, you can create your own session-handling functions for opening, closing, reading, writing, deleting, and garbage collection. To instruct PHP to use your functions for these session-related tasks, use `session_set_save_handler()` as follows:

```
session_set_save_handler ('myopen', 'myclose', 'myread', 'mywrite', 'mydelete',
➥ 'mygarbage');
```

This gives you complete flexibility over the behavior of the session management features, and you still use sessions the same way (`session_start()` and using `$_SESSION`). Thus, any existing code that uses standard session features will still work as expected.

Exam Prep Questions

1. Is it possible to pass data from PHP to JavaScript?

    A. No, because PHP is server-side, and JavaScript is client-side.

    B. No, because PHP is a loosely typed language.

    C. Yes, because JavaScript executes before PHP.

    D. Yes, because PHP can generate valid JavaScript.

    Answer **D** is correct. JavaScript, like HTML, can be dynamically generated by PHP. Answers A and B are incorrect because the answer is yes. Answer C is incorrect because PHP executes before JavaScript.

2. Is it possible to pass data from JavaScript to PHP?

    A. Yes, but not without sending another HTTP request.

    B. Yes, because PHP executes before JavaScript.

    C. No, because JavaScript is server-side, and PHP is client-side.

    D. No, because JavaScript executes before PHP.

    Answer **A** is correct. Although your instincts might lead you to believe that you cannot pass data from JavaScript to PHP, such a thing can be achieved with another HTTP request. Answer B is incorrect because PHP executing before JavaScript is not what makes this possible. This is actually the characteristic that might lead you to believe (incorrectly) that the answer is no. Answers C and D are incorrect because the answer is yes, but also because the explanations given are false.

3. Which types of form elements can be excluded from the HTTP request?

    A. text, radio, and check box

    B. text, submit, and hidden

    C. submit and hidden

    D. radio and check box

Answer **D** is correct. When not selected, both radio buttons and check boxes are excluded from the HTTP request. Answer A and B are incorrect because text boxes are always included in the request. Answer C is incorrect because hidden form elements are always included.

4. When processing the form, what is the difference between a hidden form element and a nonhidden one, such as a text box?

    A. The hidden form element does not have a name.

    B. There is no difference.

    C. The hidden form element does not have a value.

    D. The hidden form element is excluded from the request.

Answer **B** is correct. When processing a form, each form element is simply a name/value pair within one of the superglobal arrays. Answers A and C are incorrect because hidden form elements can (and should) have both a name and a value. Answer D is incorrect because hidden form elements are only excluded from the user's view, not from the HTTP request.

5. Which of the following form element names can be used to create an array in PHP?

    A. `foo`

    B. `[foo]`

    C. `foo[]`

    D. `foo[bar]`

Answer **C** is correct. PHP will create an enumerated array called `foo` that contains the values of all form elements named `foo[]` in the HTML form. Answers A, B, and D are incorrect because any subsequent form elements of the same name will overwrite the value in previous elements.

6. When an expiration date is given in a `Set-Cookie` header, what is the resulting behavior in subsequent requests?

   A. If the expiration date has expired, the cookie is not included.

   B. The behavior is the same; the expiration date is included in the Cookie header, and you can access this information in the `$_COOKIE` superglobal array.

   C. The cookie persists in memory until the browser is closed.

   D. The cookie is deleted and therefore not included in subsequent requests.

Answer **A** is correct. Answer B is incorrect because only the name and value of the cookie are included in the Cookie header. Answer C is incorrect because setting an expiration date causes a cookie to either be deleted (if the date has expired) or written to disk. Answer D is incorrect because the cookie is only deleted if the date has expired, which isn't necessarily the case.

7. If you set a cookie with either `setcookie()` or `header()`, you can immediately check to see whether the client accepted it.

   A. True, you can check the `$_COOKIE` superglobal array to see if it contains the value you set.

   B. True, but only if `register_globals` is enabled.

   C. False, you can only use `setcookie()` if you need to test for acceptance. Using `header()` does not work.

   D. False, you must wait until you receive another HTTP request to determine whether it includes the `Cookie` header.

Answer **D** is correct. The response that contains the Set-Cookie header is not sent until PHP finishes executing, so you cannot test for acceptance prior to this. Answers A and B are incorrect because the answer is false. Answer C is incorrect because using `setcookie()` and `header()` both result in the same thing: A `Set-Cookie` header is included in the response.

8. Why must you call `session_start()` prior to any output?

   A. Because it is easy to forget if not placed at the top of your scripts.

   B. Because you can no longer access the session data store after there has been output.

   C. Because `session_start()` sets some HTTP headers.

   D. Because calling `session_start()` causes the HTTP headers to be sent.

Answer **C** is correct. Answer A is incorrect because this is a technical necessity, not a best practice. Answer B is incorrect because accessing the session data store is completely independent of whether there has been any output. Answer D is incorrect because you can set other HTTP headers after a call to `session_start()`.

9. Which of the following represents the proper way to set a session variable?

    A. `$_SESSION['foo'] = 'bar';`

    B. `session_start();`

    C. `session_set_save_handler ('myopen', 'myclose', 'myread', 'mywrite', 'mydelete', 'mygarbage');`

    D. `$foo = $_SESSION['foo'];`

Answer **A** is correct. Answer B is incorrect because `session_start()` only activates PHP sessions for the current script. Answer C is incorrect because `session_set_save_handler()` allows you to override PHP's default session mechanism with your own custom functions. Answer D is incorrect; session data is being used as the value of a regular variable and is not being manipulated in any way.

10. Which of the following functions allows you to store session data in a database?

    A. `session_start();`

    B. `session_set_save_handler();`

    C. `mysql_query();`

    D. You cannot store session data in a database.

Answer **B** is correct. You can use `session_set_save_handler()` to override PHP's default session-handling functions and store session data any way you want. Answer A is incorrect because `session_start()` only activates PHP sessions for the current script. Answer C is incorrect because `mysql_query()` only executes a query with MySQL and does not affect the behavior of PHP's session mechanism. Answer D is incorrect because this statement is false.

4

Arrays

As mentioned briefly in Chapter 1, "The Basics of PHP," arrays are containers in which an arbitrary number of other data elements can be stored. If you're coming to PHP from a language such as C, the concept of array that the former adopts will be a bit different from what you're used to.

Think of an array as a "collection" of heterogeneous values, each uniquely identified by an arbitrary *key*, which can itself be either an integer numeric or string value. Thus, for example, an array could contain a floating-point value, a string, a Boolean, and even another array.

Although PHP will automatically provide a key for each value of the array if you insert them sequentially, there doesn't necessarily have to be any correlation between the keys of each elements and the order in which they appear in the array—the first item could have a key of `"a string"`, whereas the second could be `10`, and so on.

Terms You'll Need to Understand

- Array
- Key and value pairs
- Numeric arrays
- Associative arrays
- Multidimensional arrays
- Array navigation (or walking)
- Sorting
- Intersection and difference
- Data serialization

Techniques You'll Need to Master

- Creating arrays
- Handling numeric and associative keys
- Creating and handling multidimensional arrays
- Sorting arrays
- Randomizing arrays
- Intersecting arrays
- Calculating the difference between one or more arrays
- Serializing arrays

Creating Arrays

The simplest way to create an array is to use the `array` function:

```
<?

$a = array (

    '1'      => 10,
    '11'     => "test",
    'another element'

);

var_dump ($a);

?>
```

The `array` construct makes it possible to create an array while specifying the keys and the value of each pair that belongs to it, as well as the order in which they are added to it. In the specific case shown previously, the resulting array, as outputted by `var_dump()` will be as follows:

```
array(3) {
  ["1"]=>
  int(10)
  [11]=>
  string(4) "test"
  [12]=>
  string(15) "another element"
}
```

As you can see, the first element has a key of "1" and a value of 10. The second value has a key of 11 even though we specified the string "11". This is because PHP automatically converts numeric strings into the corresponding integer value. Note that, unlike what happens with string comparisons, a string value must actually be representable as an integer in order to be converted automatically—thus, for example, the string "test" does not create a key of 0.

The third value in the array has a key of 12 even though we did not specify one in our call to array(). This causes PHP to attempt and create a new key by itself by taking the highest numeric key and adding one to it. There are, however, two exceptions to this rule:

- If the array doesn't contain any element with a numeric key, an element with a key of 0 is selected instead.
- If the highest numeric key has a negative value, the new element will have a key of 0. Note that is only true as of PHP 4.3.0—prior to that version, the new element would have had a key equal to the highest numeric key plus one.

Using the Array Operator

The array operator [] is used to address an element of a particular array. For example,

```
<?

$a = array (

    '1'       => 10,
    '11'    => "test",
    'another element'

);

echo $a[11];

?>
```

The expression $a[11] returns the element of the array $a with a key that can be interpreted as the integer number 11. Note that the array operator returns a reference to the element, so you can actually use it to assign values to the element as well:

```
<?

$a[11] = 'This is a test';

?>
```

Note, however, that if you assign an array element to another variable, the assignment will still happen by value because, even though the array operator returns a reference to the element, the assignment operator will do its job by value:

```
<?

$a = array (1, 2, 3);

$b = $a[1];    // Will return 2

$b = 3;

echo $a[1]; // Will print 2

$c = &$a[1];

$c = "test";

echo $a[1]; // Will print "test"

?>
```

As you can see here, the first assignment does not cause a reference to $a[1] to be placed in $b. Instead, the value of the array element is copied into the variable, and when the latter is modified, the former remains unchanged. If the assignment takes place by reference, however, a change to the variable is also reflected in the array element.

The array operator can also be used to create an array by assigning a value to a variable as if it were an array:

```
<?

$array[1] = 1;

var_dump ($array);

?>
```

This will result in $array—which was empty at the beginning of the script—to be initialized as an array with one element whose key is 1 and whose value is 1:

```
array(1) {
  [1]=>
  int(1)
}
```

Finally, you can use the array operator to add an element to an array in sequence:

```
<?

$array[] = 1;

var_dump ($array);

?>
```

Assuming that $array was never defined, it will be reset to an array with one element with a key of 0 and a value of 1. The same notes that apply to the addition of an unkeyed element to an array using the array() construct also apply to using the array operator without specifying a key.

Counting the Number of Elements in an Array

The simplest way to count the number of elements in an array is to use the count() function:

```
<?

$array = array (
    10,
    20,
    30
);

echo count ($array); // outputs 3

?>
```

Note that you can't use count() to determine whether a variable contains an array because it returns 1 for both an array that contains one element and for any other variable that is not empty or set to Null.

Assigning Values from an Array to Multiple Variables

The list() construct makes it possible to assign the values of an array to multiple individual variables at the same time:

```
<?

$array = array (
    10,
    20,
    30
);
```

```
list ($a, $b, $c) = $array;

echo $a; // prints 10
echo $b; // prints 20
echo $c; // prints 30

?>
```

This construct works only if the array's keys are all numeric, sequential, and start from 0. Also, list() works by assigning values starting from the rightmost elements—this is not much of a problem if you're working with individual variables, but it could produce unexpected results if you're working with an array:

```
<?

$array = array (
    10,
    20,
    30
);

$a = array();

list ($a[0], $a[1], $a[2]) = $array;

var_dump ($a)

?>
```

This script will create an array that is probably not ordered the way you'd expect:

```
array(3) {
  [2]=>
  int(30)
  [1]=>
  int(20)
  [0]=>
  int(10)
}
```

Multidimensional Arrays

As we mentioned at the beginning of this chapter, an array can contain an arbitrary number of elements—including other arrays.

When an element of an array is itself an array, it can be accessed directly by appending the array operator to the array operator of the container array element:

```
<?

$array = array (

    0 => 10,
    'another array' => array (
        1 => 11,
        2 => 22)

);

echo $array['another array'][2];

?>
```

An array that contains only other arrays is referred to as a multidimensional array. For example,

```
<?

$array = array (

    array (
        10,
        20,
        30
    ),

    array (
        'a',
        'b',
        'c'
    )

);

var_dump ($array);

?>
```

The resulting array will contain two arrays, which, in turn contain three elements each. Because we didn't specify any keys, PHP will have created them for us:

```
<?

$array = array (
```

```
    array (
        10,
        20,
        30
    ),

    array (
        'a',
        'b',
        'c'
    )

);

echo $array[1][0]; // echoes 'a'
echo $array[0][2]; // echoes 30

?>
```

Navigating Arrays

The operation that is perhaps performed most often on arrays is *navigation* (or walk-ing)—the performance of a particular set of operations for each of its elements.

The simplest way to walk through an array, if you know for sure that it will always contain numeric keys starting from 0, is to simply cycle through it with a simple for loop:

```
<?

$array = array (
    10,
    20,
    30
);

for ($i = 0; $i < count ($array); $i++)
{
    echo $array[$i] * 10;
}

?>
```

In the preceding script, you'll notice that the $i < count ($array) expression is evalu-ated every time the for loop cycles. However, if the number of elements in the array is invariant, this is quite inefficient because the PHP interpreter is forced to call the count () function every time—and the result is unlikely to change. A better approach would be to move the expression count ($array) into a variable before the loop begins:

```
<?

$array = array (
    10,
    20,
    30
);

$count = count ($array);

for ($i = 0; $i < $count; $i++)
{
    echo $array[$i] * 10;
}

?>
```

This results in much better performance—but, remember, only if the number of elements in the array isn't going to change. Also, remember that you can replace the for loop with an equivalent while loop.

Using foreach

Another way of cycling through the contents of an array is to use a special construct called foreach, which works regardless of how the array is set up:

```
<?

$array = array (
    10,
    5 => 20,
    30
);

foreach ($array as $v)
{
    echo $v * 10;
}

?>
```

With this syntax, the $v variable will contain the value of every element at every step of the cycle in the order in which they appear in the array. Optionally, you can also retrieve the key:

```
<?

$array = array (
    10,
    20,
    30
);

foreach ($array as $k => $v)
{
    echo "$k = " . ($v * 10) . "\n";
}

?>
```

Although it is very practical—which makes using it extremely tempting—there is one major drawback to this construct: It works by creating a copy of the array and making all its assignments by value. This means two things: First, you can't change the value of an array element simply by modifying the value variable created by the loop construct at every step. If you want to change the value of an array element, you will have to make sure that you retrieve the key of each element as well and make the change explicitly into the array itself:

```
<?

$array = array (
    10,
    20,
    30
);

foreach ($array as $k => $v)
{
    $array[$k] = $v * 10;
}

?>
```

The second problem is the fact that the entire array must be duplicated can spell disaster for your script's performance—both in terms of CPU and memory usage, and particularly if you're dealing with a large array that is changed throughout the loop.

Using the Internal Pointer

The third way to walk through an array is to use an internal pointer that PHP automatically assigns to each array. The pointer is reset to the beginning of the array by calling the reset() function. Afterwards, each element can be retrieved by using a combination of list() and each():

```
<?

$array = array (
    10,
    20,
    30
);

reset ($array);

while (list ($k, $v) = each ($array))
{
    echo "$k = $v\n";
}

?>
```

This is the way `list()` and `each()` are most often used together. In reality, `each` actually returns an array—for example, here's what will be returned for the first row of `$array` shown previously:

```
array(4) {
  [1]=>
  int(10)
  ["value"]=>
  int(10)
  [0]=>
  int(0)
  ["key"]=>
  int(0)
}
```

The advantage of using this mechanism is that, obviously, you don't have to work on a copy of the array. Therefore, your script's performance will increase.

Using a Callback

The last way to walk through an array consists of using a *callback* function—that is, you let PHP walk through the array and call a function you designate for each element of the array. This is accomplished using the `array_walk()` function:

```
<?

$array = array (
    10,
    20,
    30
);
```

```php
function printout ($v)
{
    echo "$v\n";
}

array_walk ($array, 'printout');

?>
```

Manipulating Keys

Given the flexibility that PHP provides when assigning keys to the elements of an array, being able to manipulate the former is often as important as manipulating the latter.

The keys of an array can be extracted from an array into another array by using the `array_keys()` function:

```php
<?php

$array = array (

    1 => 10,
    'test' => 'a test string',
    200
);

$keys = array_keys ($array);

var_dump ($keys);

?>
```

By calling `array_keys()`, we cause the interpreter to return an array that contains all the keys of $array in the order in which the respective elements appear in the array itself:

```
array(3) {
  [0]=>
  int(1)
  [1]=>
  string(4) "test"
  [2]=>
  int(2)
}
```

Checking if an Element Exists

There are at least two ways to directly determine whether an element of an array exists. The simplest is to use is_set:

```php
<?php

$array = array (

    1 => 10,
    'test' => 'a test string',
    200
);

if (isset ($array[2]))
{
    echo 'Element 2 is : ' . $array[2];
}

?>
```

This is simple enough and quite useful whenever you need to access an element of an array (or, for that matter, any variable) and you're not sure that it's already been set.

Another possibility consists of using the array_key_exists() function:

```php
<?php

$array = array (

    1 => 10,
    'test' => 'a test string',
    200
);

if (array_key_exists ($array, 2))
{
    echo 'Element 2 is : ' . $array[2];
}

?>
```

The net effect of using this function instead of isset() is the same—the only difference being that the latter is a language construct and, therefore, probably a bit faster than the former.

Changing the Array of Keys

The `array_change_key_case()` function can be used to change the case of an array's keys:

```php
<?php

$array = array (

    1 => 10,
    'test' => 'a test string',
    200
);

$arr_2 = array_change_key_case ($array, CASE_UPPER);

var_dump ($arr_2);

?>
```

As you can see, `array_change_key_case()` returns a copy of the original array (which translates in a performance impact if you're dealing with a large array) whose keys have all been changed to the specified case. The second parameter of the call determines the new case of the keys. `CASE_UPPER` changes the case to uppercase, whereas `CASE_LOWER` does the opposite.

Sorting an Array by Its Keys

As we mentioned at the beginning, there is no predefined relationship between the key of an element and the element's position in the array. This is not always a desirable situation, however, and you might want to be able to actually ensure that the elements of the array are sorted according to their keys. This can be accomplished by using one of two functions—`ksort()` and `krsort()`:

```php
<?php

$array = array (

    1 => 10,
    'test' => 'a test string',
    200
);

echo "Sorting in ascending order: \n";

ksort ($array);
```

```
var_dump ($array);

echo "Sorting in descending order: \n";

krsort ($array);

var_dump ($array);

?>
```

The `ksort()` function causes the array to be ordered in ascending order based on its keys:

```
Sorting in ascending order:
array(3) {
  ["test"]=>
  string(13) "a test string"
  [1]=>
  int(10)
  [2]=>
  int(200)
}
```

`krsort()`, on the other hand, performs the exact opposite operation, sorting the array in descending order based on its keys:

```
Sorting in descending order:
array(3) {
  [2]=>
  int(200)
  [1]=>
  int(10)
  ["test"]=>
  string(13) "a test string"
}
```

A number of options can be specified as the last parameter when calling either one of these functions to determine how the sorting is performed:

- `SORT_REGULAR` (default)—Causes the array to be sorted according to the normal rules that apply to comparison operations
- `SORT_NUMERIC`—Causes the comparison operations to be performed as if all the keys were numeric
- `SORT_STRING`—Causes the comparison operations to be performed as if all the keys were strings

These flags, which indeed apply to all array sorting operations, can significantly affect the outcome of a call to `ksort()` or `krsort()`. For example,

```php
<?php

$array = array (

    1 => 10,
    'test' => 'a test string',
    200
);

echo "Sorting in ascending order: \n";

ksort ($array, SORT_STRING);

var_dump ($array);

?>
```

If you execute this script, you will obtain a very different result from the one previously because all the keys will be converted to strings and compared as such:

```
array(3) {
  [1]=>
  int(10)
  [2]=>
  int(200)
  ["test"]=>
  string(13) "a test string"
}
```

Manipulating Arrays

The amount of functions that manipulate arrays in PHP is staggering—a testament to just how powerful and popular these elements of the language are.

The most common operation that you will want to perform on an array will probably be to sort it—there are a number of ways that you can go about it.

The simplest way to sort is to use the `sort()` or `rsort()` functions, which behave in exactly the same way as `ksort()` and `krsort()` previously except that the sorting is done on the values of each element rather than on the keys.

The only problem with using either one of these functions is that they do not maintain the association between keys and values. For example,

```php
<?php

$array = array (

    1 => 10,
    'test' => 'a test string',
```

```
    200
);

sort ($array);

var_dump ($array);

?>
```

This script *will* sort the elements of $array, but the end result might not be what you were expecting:

```
array(3) {
  [0]=>
  string(13) "a test string"
  [1]=>
  int(10)
  [2]=>
  int(200)
}
```

As you can see, the keys have been completely lost. If you want to maintain the associativity of the array, you will have to use asort() (for sorting in ascending order) and arsort() (for sorting in descending order):

```
<?php

$array = array (

    1 => 10,
    'test' => 'a test string',
    200
);

asort ($array);

var_dump ($array);

?>
```

This will result in the keys being saved and the order being changed as appropriate:

```
array(3) {
  ["test"]=>
  string(13) "a test string"
  [1]=>
  int(10)
  [2]=>
  int(200)
}
```

Note that all the parameters that could be passed to `ksort()` and `krsort()` can also be passed to any of the other sorting functions we have examined this far.

Sorting Multidimensional Arrays

When dealing with multidimensional arrays, sorting becomes a slightly more complex problem because each of the sub-arrays must also be sorted. If you use any of the sorting functions shown so far on a multidimensional array, only the main array will be sorted—the sub-arrays will remain untouched (and this might be what you're after).

If you want the sub-arrays to be sorted as well—independently of each other—you will have to do the honors by hand yourself:

```php
<?php

$array = array (

    array (11 => 10, 5 => 0, 3 => "a", 100),
    array (-1, 30, true, "test")

);

$count = count ($array);

for ($i = 0; $i < $count; $i++)
{
    sort ($array[$i]);
}

?>
```

PHP offers a function, called `array_multisort()`, that can come in handy when you want to sort an array in relation to the contents of another. This function behaves similarly to the SQL ORDER BY clause with each array passed to be interpreted as one column in a set of rows. Sounds confusing, doesn't it? Let's look at an example.

Suppose that you have a list of people and their ages in two arrays:

```php
$array = array (

    array ('Jack', 'John', 'Marco', 'Daniel'),
    array (21, 23, 29, 44)

);
```

If you want to sort the names alphabetically, for example, and maintain the correspondence between each element in the first array with each element of the second—so that after the sorting operation, the string `Daniel` will be in the same position as the number 44—`array_multisort()` is the function for you:

```php
<?php

$array = array (

    array ('Jack', 'John', 'Marco', 'Daniel'),
    array (21, 23, 29, 44)

);

array_multisort ($array[0], $array[1]);

var_dump ($array);

?>
```

This will cause the elements of `$array[1]` to be sorted in the same way as those of `$array[0]`:

```
array(2) {
  [0]=>
  array(4) {
    [0]=>
    string(6) "Daniel"
    [1]=>
    string(4) "Jack"
    [2]=>
    string(4) "John"
    [3]=>
    string(5) "Marco"
  }
  [1]=>
  array(4) {
    [0]=>
    int(44)
    [1]=>
    int(21)
    [2]=>
    int(23)
    [3]=>
    int(29)
  }
}
```

As you can see, the string `Daniel` is now first in `$array[0]`, and the value `44` has been moved accordingly. If two values in the first array have the same value, the corresponding values in the second one will be sorted alphabetically as well:

```php
<?php

$array = array (

    array ('Jack', 'John', 'Marco', 'Marco', 'Daniel'),
    array (21, 23, 29, 11, 44)

);

array_multisort ($array[0], $array[1]);

var_dump ($array);

?>
```

This will result in the two values that correspond to Marco to be rearranged according to normal sorting rules:

```
array(2) {
  [0]=>
  array(5) {
    [0]=>
    string(6) "Daniel"
    [1]=>
    string(4) "Jack"
    [2]=>
    string(4) "John"
    [3]=>
    string(5) "Marco"
    [4]=>
    string(5) "Marco"
  }
  [1]=>
  array(5) {
    [0]=>
    int(44)
    [1]=>
    int(21)
    [2]=>
    int(23)
    [3]=>
    int(11)
    [4]=>
    int(29)
  }
}
```

You can even specify how the sorting takes place by passing two optional parameters after each array. The first determines how the sorting comparisons are performed (and accepts the same flags as the other sorting operations we have seen), whereas the second one determines whether the sorting is done in ascending (SORT_ASC) or descending (SORT_DESC) order.

It's important to keep in mind that using array_multisort() is *not* the same as sorting an array recursively as we did at the beginning of this section.

Randomizing Arrays

It's often useful to extract a random value from an array. This can be accomplished by using the array_rand() function, which returns the index of one or more elements picked at random:

```php
<?php

$array = array ('Jack', 'John', 'Marco', 'Marco', 'Daniel');

echo array_rand ($array, 1);


?>
```

In this case, we specified that only one element should be returned; therefore, we'll receive a single value. (It was 4 in my case, corresponding to the "Daniel" element.) Had we specified more than one element, the result would have been returned as an array of keys.

The array_rand() function corresponds a bit to saying "pick a card at random from the deck." What if, however, you want to shuffle the deck and change the order of the array elements in a random way? That's where the shuffle() function comes into play. In fact, let's look at this simple example, which creates an array of cards (each composed of one letter to identify the suit and one character to identify the face itself):

```php
<?php

$suits = "CDSH";
$cards = "A234567890JQK";

$suit_count = 4;
$card_count = 13;

// Create the deck

$deck = array();

for ($i = 0; $i < $suit_count; $i++)
{
```

```
        for ($j = 0; $j < $card_count; $j++)
        {
            $deck[] = $suits{$i} . $cards{$j};
        }
    }

var_dump ($deck);

// Now shuffle the deck

shuffle ($deck);
var_dump ($deck);

?>
```

This script starts by creating a deck in which the cards are placed in sequence (for example; CA, C2, C3, and so on) and then calls the `shuffle()` function to randomize the order in which the items appear in the array. The output is too long to show here, but you could definitely run a solitaire game just by picking out each element of the shuffled deck in turn.

Merging Arrays

Another frequently needed array-manipulation feature is merging two or more arrays together. This is done by calling the `array_merge()` function:

```
<?php

$a = array (10, 20, 30, 40);
$b = array (10, 20, 30, 40);

$array = array_merge ($a, $b);

var_dump ($array);

?>
```

This results in the $a and $b arrays being appended to each other in the order in which they appear in the call to `array_merge()` and being stored in a new array:

```
array(8) {
  [0]=>
  int(10)
  [1]=>
  int(20)
  [2]=>
  int(30)
  [3]=>
  int(40)
```

```
 [4]=>
 int(10)
 [5]=>
 int(20)
 [6]=>
 int(30)
 [7]=>
 int(40)
}
```

As you can see here, the two arrays are simply meshed together, and any values that appear in both arrays are added to the end. This, however, only happens if they have numeric keys—if they are associative elements with string keys, the element in the second array ends up in the result:

```php
<?php

$a = array ('a' => 10, 20, 30, 40);
$b = array ('a' => 20, 20, 30, 40);

$array = array_merge ($a, $b);

var_dump ($array);

?>
```

The preceding example will print this result:

```
array(7) {
  ["a"]=>
  int(20)
  [0]=>
  int(20)
  [1]=>
  int(30)
  [2]=>
  int(40)
  [3]=>
  int(20)
  [4]=>
  int(30)
  [5]=>
  int(40)
}
```

As you can see, the value of the 'a' element in $b ends up in the result array. If this behavior is not what you're looking for, you can use array_merge_recursive(), which takes elements with the same string keys and combines them into an array inside the value it returns:

```php
<?php

$a = array ('a' => 10, 20, 30, 40);
$b = array ('a' => 20, 20, 30, 40);

$array = array_merge_recursive ($a, $b);

var_dump ($array);

?>
```

This results in the following array:

```
array(7) {
  ["a"]=>
  array(2) {
    [0]=>
    int(10)
    [1]=>
    int(20)
  }
  [0]=>
  int(20)
  [1]=>
  int(30)
  [2]=>
  int(40)
  [3]=>
  int(20)
  [4]=>
  int(30)
  [5]=>
  int(40)
}
```

In this case, `$a['a']` and `$b['a']` are combined together into the `$array['a']` array.

Intersection and Difference

If you want to extract all the elements that are common to two or more arrays, you can use the `array_intersect()`:

```php
<?php

$a = array ('a' => 20, 36, 40);
$b = array ('b' => 20, 30, 40);
```

```
$array = array_intersect ($a, $b);

var_dump ($array);

?>
```

Here's the output:

```
array(2) {
  ["a"]=>
  int(20)
  [1]=>
  int(40)
}
```

As you can see, this function only checks whether the values are the same—the keys are ignored (although the key of the leftmost array is preserved). If you want to include them in the check, you should use `array_intersect_assoc()` instead:

```
<?php

$a = array ('a' => 20, 36, 40);
$b = array ('b' => 20, 30, 40);

$array = array_intersect_assoc ($a, $b);

var_dump ($array);

?>
```

In this case, the result will be a one-element array because the two 20 values in $a and $b have different keys:

```
array(1) {
  [1]=>
  int(40)
}
```

If you want to calculate the difference between two or more arrays—that is, elements that only appear in one of the arrays but not in any of the others—you will need to use either `array_diff()` or `array_diff_assoc()` instead.

Serializing Arrays

Given their flexibility, arrays are often used to store all sorts of information, and it is handy to be able to save their contents at the end of a script and retrieve them later on. This is done through a process, known as "serialization," in which the contents of an array are rendered in a format that can later be used to rebuild the array in memory.

In PHP, serialization is taken care of by two functions:

- `serialize()` renders the array in a format that can be safely saved to any container (such as a database field or a file) capable of handling textual content.

- `unserialize()` takes a serialized input and rebuilds the array in memory.

Using these two functions is very easy:

```
<?php

$a = array ('a' => 20, 36, 40);

$saved = serialize ($a);

// Your script may stop here if you save the contents
// of $saved in a file or database field

$restored = unserialize ($saved);

?>
```

The serialization functionality is very flexible and will be able to save everything that is stored in your array—except, of course, for resource variables, which will have to be recreated when the array is unserialized.

Exam Prep Questions

1. Which of the following types can be used as an array key? (Select three.)

    A. Integer
    B. Floating-point
    C. Array
    D. Object
    E. Boolean

Answers **A**, **B**, and **E** are correct. A Boolean value will be converted to either 0 if it is false or 1 if it is true, whereas a floating-point value will be truncated to its integer equivalent. Arrays and objects, however, cannot be used under any circumstance.

2. Which of the following functions can be used to sort an array by its keys in descending order?

    A. `sort`

    B. `rsort`

    C. `ksort`

    D. `krsort`

    E. `reverse_sort`

    D is correct. The `sort()` and `rsort()` functions operate on values, whereas `ksort()` sorts in ascending order and `reverse_sort()` is not a PHP function.

3. What will the following script output?

```php
<?php

$a = array ('a' => 20, 1 => 36, 40);

array_rand ($a);

echo $a[0];

?>
```

    A. A random value from $a

    B. `'a'`

    C. `20`

    D. `36`

    E. Nothing

    Only **E** is correct. The `$a` array doesn't have any element with a numeric key of zero, and the `array_rand()` function does not change the keys of the array's elements—only their order.

Questions of this type are in the exam not to trick you, but rather as a way to test your ability to troubleshoot a problem. In this particular example, a developer who is well versed in PHP recognizes the problem immediately, whereas a less experienced programmer will be sidetracked by thinking that something is wrong with the function being called. After all, these kinds of bugs, usually caused by distraction or typos, are quite common in real-life code.

5

Strings and Regular Expressions

Terms You'll Need to Understand

- The == and === operators
- Regular expression
- PCRE

Techniques You'll Need to Master

- Formatting strings
- Comparing strings
- Modifying string contents
- Using regular expressions for pattern matching and extraction.
- Joining and splitting strings

The Web is largely a text-oriented environment. Data is submitted to websites in the form of text strings, and the response (be it in HTML, XML, or even an image format) is generally text as well. Accordingly, being able to analyze and manipulate text is a core skill of any PHP programmer.

Comparing Strings

In this section, you will learn how to test whether two strings are equal, or whether one string exists inside of another string.

Comparison with == and ===

The most basic way of comparing any two entities in PHP is using the == operator (called the *is equal* operator). When the == operator tests the equivalence of two entities, it first reduces them to a common type. This often causes unexpected results. For example, the following code outputs $a and $b are equal:

```
$a = 'Hello World';
$b = 0;
if($a == $b) {
  print "\$a and \$b are equal\n";
} else {
  print "\$a and \$b are not equal\n";
}
```

The reason this happens is that $a is a string type and $b is an integer, so the Zend Engine needs to convert them to a common type for comparison. == is a weak operator, so it converts to the more lenient type, namely integer. The integer representation of 'Hello World' is 0, so $a == $b is true. == should only be used to compare strings if you are certain that both its operands are in fact strings.

PHP also provides the stronger equivalence operator === (called the *is identical* operator). Whereas the == was too weak to be useful in many situations, === is often too strong. === performs no type-homogenization, and requires that both operands be of the same type before a comparison can be successful. Thus, the following code outputs $a and $b are not equal:

```
$a = 1;
$b = "1";
if($a === $b) {
  print "\$a and \$b are equal\n";
} else {
  print "\$a and \$b are not equal\n";
}
```

This result occurs because $a is internally held as an integer, whereas $b, by virtue of its being quoted, is a string.

Thus, === can be dangerous to use if you are not certain that both operands are strings.

> **Tip**
>
> You can force a variable to be cast to strings by the use of casts. Thus,
>
> ```
> if( (string) $a === (string) $b) { ... }
> ```
>
> will convert both $a and $b to strings before performing the conversion. This produces the results you expect, but is a bit clumsy—using the strcmp family of functions is generally preferred.

Using `strcmp` and Friends

The preferred way of comparing two entities as strings is to use the `strcmp()` function. `strcmp()` takes two arguments and compares them *lexigraphically* (also known as *dictionary ordering*, as it is the same logic used in sorting words in a dictionary). `strcmp()` returns 0 if the two strings are identical. Thus this code, which gave us trouble before, will correctly output that `$a` and `$b` are the same:

```
$a = 1;
$b = "1";
if(strcmp($a, $b) == 0) {
  print "\$a and \$b are the same\n";
} else {
  print "\$a and \$b are different\n";
}
```

If its two operands are not the same, `strcmp()` will return -1 if the first operand would appear before the second in a dictionary, and 1 if the first operand would appear after the second in a dictionary. This behavior makes it very useful for sorting arrays of words. In fact, the following two bits of code will sort the array `$colors` in the same fashion (in dictionary order):

```
$colors = array("red", "blue", "green");
sort($colors, SORT_STRING);
```

and

```
$colors = array("red", "blue", "green");
usort($colors, 'strcmp');
```

By itself, this is not very useful. (`sort()` should be preferred over `usort()` when performing equivalent tasks), but `strcmp()` has some sibling functions that perform similar tasks.

`strcasecmp()` is identical to `strcmp()` except that it performs comparisons that are not case sensitive. This means that the following code that will output `$a` is the same as HELLO, modulo case:

```
$a = 'hello';
if(strcasecmp($a, 'HELLO')) {
  print "\$a is the same as HELLO, modulo case\n";
}
```

Also, RED will come after blue when sorted via `strcasecmp()`, whereas with `strcmp()`, RED will come before blue.

Matching Portions of Strings

You've seen how to match strings exactly, but sometimes you only need to match a portion of a string. When only a portion of a string is considered, it is referred to as a *substring*. Specifically, a substring is any portion of a string. For example, PHP is a substring of the string PHP is a scripting language.

Matching Leading Substrings

To match only the leading portion of strings, PHP provides the strncmp() family of functions. strncmp() and strncasecmp() are identical to strcmp() and strcasecmp(), but both take a third parameter, $n, that instructs PHP to compare only the first $n characters of both strings. Thus strncmp('figure1.gif', 'figure2.gif', 6) will return 0 (equal) because only the first six characters of each string is compared.

Matching Substrings at Arbitrary Offsets

If you need to determined simply whether a substring exists *anywhere* inside a given string, you should use strstr(). strstr() takes as its first argument a string to be searched (often called the *subject*), and as its second the substring to search for (often called the *search pattern*). If strstr() succeeds, it will return the searched for substring and all text following it; otherwise, it returns false.

Here is a use of strstr() to determine whether the word PHP appears in the string $string:

```
if(strstr($string, 'PHP') !== FALSE) {
  // do something
}
```

If you want to search for a substring irrespective of case, you can use stristr(). Here is a check to see if any forms of 'PHP' (including 'php', 'Php', and so on) appear in $string:

```
if(stristr($string, 'PHP') !== FALSE) {
  // do something
}
```

If instead of the actual string you would like the position of the match returned to you, you can use strpos(). strpos() works similarly to strstr(), with two major differences:

- Instead of returning the substring containing the match, strpos() returns the character offset of the start of the match.
- strpos() accepts an optional third parameter that allows you to start looking at a particular offset.

Here is a sample usage of strpos() to find every starting position of the substring 'PHP' in a search subject $string.

```
$offset = 0;
$match_pos = array();
while(($offset = strpos($string, 'PHP', $offset)) !== FALSE) {
  $match_pos[] = $offset;
}
```

strpos() also has a not case-sensitive form, stripos(), that behaves in a similar fashion.

> **Tip**
>
> Because the first character in a string is at position 0, you should always use === to test whether a match from strpos() succeeded or failed.

If you need to match from the end of your subject backwards, you can do so with strchr(), strrpos(), or strripos(). strrpos() and strripos() behave identically to strpos() and stripos() with the exception that they start at the end of the subject string and that the search pattern can only be a single character. strrchr() behaves like strstr(), returning the matched character and the rest of the subject following it, but it also requires a single character search pattern and operates starting at the end of the subject (this is in contrast with the majority of strr* functions, which take full strings for all their arguments).

Formatting Strings

Specifying specific formats for strings is largely a leftover from compiled languages such as C, where string interpolation and static typing make it more difficult to take a collection of variables and assemble them into a string. For the most part, PHP will do all of this for you. For example, most string formatting looks like this:

```
$name = 'George';
$age = 30;
print "$name is $age years old.";
```

When variables are placed inside a double-quoted string, they are automatically expanded. PHP knows how to convert numbers into strings as well, so $age is correctly expanded as well.

Occasionally, however, you need to perform more complex formatting. This includes the padding of numbers with 0s (for example, displaying 05 instead of 5), limiting the printed precision of floating point numbers, forcing right-justification, or limiting the number of characters printed in a particular string.

printf Formats

The basic function for formatting is printf(). printf() takes a format string and a list of arguments. It then passes through the formatting string, substituting special tokens contained therein with the correctly formatted arguments.

Formatting tokens are denoted with a %. In their simplest form, this is followed directly by a *type specifier* from Table 5.1.

Table 5.1   `printf()` **Format Specifiers**

Specifier	Format
b	The argument is treated as an integer and is presented as an integer in binary form.
c	The argument is treated as an integer and is presented as the ASCII character for that value.
d	The argument is treated as an integer and presented as a signed integer.
u	The argument is treated as an integer and presented as an unsigned integer.
f	The argument is treated as a floating-point number and presented as a floating-point number.
o	The argument is treated as an integer and presented as its octal representation.
x	The argument is treated as an integer and presented as a hexadecimal number (using lowercase letters).
X	The argument is treated as an integer and presented as a hexadecimal number (using uppercase letters).

Thus, the preceding simple code block that prints $name and $age can be rewritten as follows:

```
printf("%s is %d years old", $name, $age);
```

By itself, this is not terribly useful. Though it might be slightly more readable than using interpolated variables (especially to people coming from a C or Java background), it is also slower and not more flexible.

The usefulness of the formatting functions comes via the format modifiers that can be added between the % and the format specifier, from right to left:

- A floating-point precision, given by a . followed by the desired precision that says how many decimal places should be displayed for a floating point number. Note that this will round numbers to the specified precision.
- A field width that dictates how many characters minimum should be displayed for this token. For example, to guarantee that at least eight characters are allotted for an integer, you would use the format specifier "%8d". By default, blank spaces are used to pad the results.
- To left-justify a formatting, a - can be added to the format.
- Instead of using blank spaces, an expansion can be padded with 0s by preceding the width-specifier with a 0. Thus, if you are printing time in 24-hour notation (such that one o'clock is printed as 01:00), you can use the following:

```
printf("%02d:%02d", $hour, $minute);
```

Optionally, a different character can be specified by escaping it with a ʼ. So to pad all your numbers with xxx, you would use

```
printf("%'xd", $number);
```

`printf()` **Family Functions**

PHP has a small collection of formatting functions that are differentiated from each other by how they take their arguments and how they handle their results.

The basic function (which you saw previously) is `printf()`. `printf()` takes a format string and a variable number of arguments that it uses to fill out the format string. It outputs the result.

`fprintf()` is identical to `printf()`, except that instead of writing output to the standard display stream, it writes output to an arbitrary stream resource specified as the first parameter.

`sprintf()` is identical to `printf()`, but instead of outputting its results, it returns them as a string.

`vprintf()` takes its arguments as a single array (instead of a variable number of individual arguments) and outputs the result. This is useful when you are passed a variable number of arguments—for example, via `call_user_func_array()` or `func_get_args()`.

`vsprintf()` is identical to `vprintf()`, except that instead of outputting its result, it returns it as a string.

Table 5.2 is a complete listing of all the formatting functions, with a list of the args they take and where their result is sent (as output, to an arbitrary stream, or to a string).

Table 5.2   **Formatting Functions**

Function	Args	Result
printf	format, args	writes output
sprintf	format, args	returns result
vprintf	format, array of args	writes output
vsprintf	format, array of args	returns result
fprintf	stream resource, format, args	writes output to stream

Extracting Data from Strings

When dealing with data that comes in from an external source (for example, read from a file or submitted via a form), complex data is often packed into strings and needs to be extracted. Common examples include decomposing phone numbers, credit card numbers, and email addresses into their base components. PHP provides both basic string functions for efficiently extracting data in fixed formats, as well as regular expression facilities for matching more complex data.

Extracting Substrings by Offset

To extract a substring by offset, you can use the `substr()` function. `substr()` works by taking a string (the subject), an offset from the beginning of the string from which to start, and an optional length (by default, the remainder of the string from which the start offset is grabbed).

For example, to get all of `$string` except for the first character, you can use the following:

```
$result = substr($string, 1);
```

or to grab the first eight characters of a string, you can use this code:

```
$result = substr($string, 0, 8);
```

For a more nontrivial example, consider this code that grabs the local part of an email address (the part before the @ character) by using `strpos()` to find the @ symbol and `substr()` to extract the substring preceding it:

```
$local_part = substr($email, 0, strpos($email, '@'));
```

If you need to grab a substring at the end of your subject, you can use a negative offset to indicate that your match is relative to the end of a string. For example, to grab the last four characters of a string, you can do the following:

```
$result = substr($email, -4);
```

If you need to only access individual characters in a string, you can use curly braces ({}) to access the string's characters by offsets. For example, to iterate over every character in a string and capitalize the odd numbered characters, you can do the following:

```
$len = strlen($string);
for($i = 0; $i < $len; $i++) {
  if($i % 2) {
    $string{$i} = strtoupper($string{$i});
  }
}
```

Extracting Formatted Data

Real-world data extraction tasks often involve strings that have vague formats. Complex data extraction usually requires the use of regular expressions (covered later in this chapter), but if the data is of a format that can be specified with a `printf()` formatting string, you can use `sscanf()` to extract the data.

For example, to match IP address/port number pairings of the form `127.0.0.1:6137`, you can use the format `"%d.%d.%d.%d:%d"`. That can be used with `sscanf()` as follows:

```
$parts = sscanf($string, "%d.%d.%d.%d:%d");
```

If $string is `127.0.0.1:6137`, $parts will be filled out thusly:

```
Array
(
    [0] => 127
    [1] => 0
    [2] => 0
    [3] => 1
    [4] => 6137
)
```

Though flexible, `sscanf()` parsing is a bit fragile: The pattern must match exactly (modulo whitespace) at the beginning of the subject string.

Modifying Strings

In this section, you will see how to modify strings by replacing substrings, both by the offset of where you want to perform the replacement and by simple pattern match (for example, replacing all occurrences of 'foo' with 'bar').

Modifying Substrings by Offset

To replace a substring in a subject string, you can use the `substr_replace()` function. `substr_replace()`'s first argument is a subject string; its second a replacement string; its third the offset to start the replacement at; and its optional fourth argument is the length of the subject substring to replace.

To illustrate this, consider how to X out all but the last four digits of a credit card number. Here is code to perform this with `substr_replace()`:

```
$len = strlen($ccnum);
$newnum = substr_replace($ccnum, str_repeat('X', $len -4), 0, $len - 4);
```

First, you find the length of the credit card number in question, and then you replace the first $len - 4 characters with an equal number of X's.

Replacing Substrings

Another common string modification task is replacing all occurrences of one substring with another. The preferred function for doing this is `str_replace()`. `str_replace()` takes as its first argument a string to be matched, and as its second the string to substitute in. Its third parameter is the subject on which all this replacement should occur. For example, to replace all occurrences of `:)` with the image link `<img src="/smiley.png"/>`, you can use the following replacement:

```
$new_subject = str_replace(':)', '<img src="/smiley.png"/>', $subject);
```

Of course, you often need to do not case-sensitive substitutions. For example, if you
need to reverse the action of nl2br() and replace all HTML <br> line breaks with
newlines, you need to match <br> not case sensitively. str_ireplace() supplies this
semantic, enabling the search strings to be matched irrespective of case. Here is a function br2nl() illustrating that:

```
function br2nl($subject)
{
  return str_ireplace("<br>", "\n", $subject);
}
```

Both str_replace() and str_ireplace() also accept arrays for all their parameters.
When arrays are passed for the pattern and replacement, all the replacements are executed with that one call. If an array of subjects is passed, the indicated replacements will be
performed on each in turn. Here you can see this array functionality used to substitute a
couple of emoticons in one pass:

```
$emoticons = array( ':)' => '<img src="/smiley.png"/>',
                    ';)' => '<img src="/wink.png"/>',
                    ':(' => '<img src="/frown.png"/>');
$new_subject = str_replace(array_keys($emoticons),
                    array_values($emoticons), $subject);
```

Regular Expressions

The most powerful tools in the string manipulation toolbox are regular expressions
(often abbreviated *regexps*). Regular expressions provide a robust language for specifying
patterns in strings and extracting or replacing identified portions of text.

The regular expressions in PHP come in two flavors: PCRE and POSIX. PCRE regular
expressions are so named because they use the Perl Compatible Regular Expression
library to provide regexps with the same syntax and semantics as those in Perl. POSIX
regular expressions support standard POSIX-extended regular expression syntax. The
POSIX regular expression functions (the ereg_ family of functions and split()) are
slower than their PCRE equivalents, not-binary safe, less flexible, and in general their use
is discouraged in favor of the PCRE functions.

Basic PCRE Syntax

A regular expression pattern is a string consisting of plain text and pattern metacharacters. The regexp metacharacters define the type and number of characters that can match
a particular part of a pattern.

The most basic set of metacharacters are the character classes, which allow a pattern
to match multiple characters simultaneously. The basic character classes are shown in
Table 5.3.

Table 5.3 **PCRE Base Character Classes**

Metacharacter	Characters Matched
\d	Digits 0–9
\D	Anything not a digit
\w	Any alphanumeric character or an underscore (_)
\W	Anything not an alphanumeric character or an underscore
\s	Any whitespace (spaces, tabs, newlines)
\S	Any nonwhitespace character
.	Any character except for a newline

The basic character class metacharacters each match a single character. Thus, to make them useful in patterns, you need to be able to specify how many times they must match. To do this, PCRE supports enumeration operators. The enumeration operators are shown in Table 5.4.

Table 5.4 **PCRE Enumerators**

Operator	Meaning
?	Occurs 0 or 1 time
*	Occurs 0 or more times
+	Occurs 1 or more times
{,n}	Occurs at most n times
{m,}	Occurs m or more times
{m,n}	Occurs between m and n times

Putting these together, you can form basic patterns such as, 'matches a US ZIP+4': \d{5}-\d{4}. Notice that the - character is in the pattern. If a nonmetacharacter appears in the pattern, it must be matched exactly.

To test to see if a string $subject matches this pattern, you use preg_match() as follows:

```
if(preg_match("/\d{5}-\d{4}/", $subject)) {
  // matches a ZIP+4
}
```

preg_match()'s first argument is the pattern, and the second argument is the subject string. Notice that the pattern itself is enclosed in forward slashes. PCRE supports arbitrary delimiters for patterns, but be aware that the delimiter character must be escaped within the pattern.

Unlike sscanf() format matches, a preg_match() will match anywhere it can in the subject string. If you want to specify that the pattern must start matching immediately at the beginning of the subject, you should use the positional anchor ^. You can also match the end of a string with the positional anchor $. Thus, to match a string only if it is *exactly* a U.S. ZIP+4, with no leading or trailing information, you can use the following

```
if(preg_match("/^\d{5}-\d{4}$/", $subject)) {
  // matches a ZIP+4 exactly
}
```

You can create your own character classes by enclosing the desired characters in brackets ([]). Ranges are allowed. Thus to create a character class that matches only the digits 2 through 9, you can use

```
[2-9]
```

You could use this in a regular expression to capture U.S. phone numbers as follows:

```
/[2-9]\d{2}-[2-9]\d{2}-\d{4}/
```

U.S. area codes and exchanges cannot begin with a 0 or a 1, so this regexp avoids them by looking for a digit between 2 and 9 followed by any two digits.

Patterns can have aspects of their base behavior changed by appending modifiers after the closing delimiter. A list of common pattern modifiers is shown in Table 5.5.

Table 5.5 **PCRE Pattern Modifiers**

Modifier	Meaning
i	Matches not case sensitively
m	Enables positional anchors to match at any newline in a subject string
s	Enables . to match newlines
x	Enables comments and whitespace in regexps
u	Treats data as UTF-8

Extracting Data with Regular Expressions

Usually you will want to do more than assert that a subject matches a pattern; you will also want to extract the portions of the subject that match the pattern. To capture pieces of patterns, you must group the portions of the pattern you want to capture with parentheses. For example, to capture the two components of a ZIP+4 code into separate matches, you need to group them individually into *subpatterns* as follows:

```
/(\d{5})-(\d{4})/
```

After you've specified your capture subpatterns, you can read their matches by passing an array as the third parameter to preg_match(). The subpattern matches will be stored in the match array by their pattern number, which is determined by numbering the subpatterns left-to-right by the position of their opening parenthesis. To illustrate, if you execute the following code:

```
$string = 'My zipcode is 21797-2046';
if(preg_match("/(\d{5})-(\d{4})/", $string, $matches)) {
  print_r($matches);
}
```

you will get this output:

```
Array
(
    [0] => 21797-2046
    [1] => 21797
    [2] => 2046
)
```

Note that $matches[0] contains the portion of $string matched by the pattern as a whole, whereas the two subpatterns are accessible by their pattern numbers. Also note that because the pattern is not anchored with ^, it is not a problem that the subject does not begin with the ZIP Code and the match can commence in the middle of the string.

> **Tip**
>
> preg_match() only matches the first occurrence of its regexp. To execute a global match that returns all matches in the subject, you can use preg_match_all().

Pattern Replacement with Regular Expressions

Regular expressions also allow you to perform replacements on subject strings. Performing replacements with regexps is similar to using str_replace() except that instead of a fixed string being searched for, an arbitrary regular expression pattern can be used.

To perform a regular expression substitution, use the preg_replace() function. Its first argument is a regular expression that should match the text you want to replace. Its second argument is the replacement text, which can either be a string literal or can contain references to subpatterns as \n (where n is the subpattern number). Its third argument is the subject string to operate on.

Thus, if you match email addresses with /(\S+)@(\S+)/, you can sanitize them (removing the @ to reduce address harvesting by spammers) by performing the following substitution:

```
$new_subject = preg_replace("/(\S+)@(\S+)/", '\1 at \2', $subject);
```

This code will convert addresses such as 'license@php.net' to 'license at php.net'.

Splitting Strings into Components

PHP provides you three main options for taking a string and separating it into components: explode(), split(), and preg_split().

`explode()` is the simplest of the three options. It enables a string to be split into components based on a completely static delimiter. A typical usage of this would be to extract all the information from a UNIX systems `/etc/passwd` file, as shown here:

```
$info = array();
$lines = file("/etc/passwd");
foreach($lines as $line) {
  $info[] = explode(':', $line);
}
```

Because its matching logic is simple and it involves no regular expressions, `explode()` is the fastest of the three splitting methods. When possible, you should prefer it over `split()` and `preg_split()`.

`split()` is a POSIX extended regular expression function, and should in general be eschewed for `preg_split()`, which is more flexible and just as fast.

`preg_split()` allows you to break up a string using a regexp for your delimiter. This provides you a great deal of flexibility. For example, to split on any amount of white-space, you can use the following regexp:

```
$parts = preg_split("/\s+/", $subject);
```

`preg_split()`'s use of regular expressions makes it more flexible but a bit slower than `explode()`. Use it when you have complex decomposition tasks to carry out.

Exam Prep Questions

1. Given

   ```
   $email = 'bob@example.com';
   ```

   which code block will output `example.com`?

   A. `print substr($email, -1 * strrpos($email, '@'));`

   B. `print substr($email, strrpos($email, '@'));`

   C. `print substr($email, strpos($email, '@') + 1);`

   D. `print strstr($email, '@');`

   Answer **C** is correct. `strpos()` identifies the position of the @ character in the string. To capture only the domain part of the address, you must advance one place to the first character after the @.

2. Which question will replace markup such as `img=/smiley.png` with `<img src="/smiley.png">`?

   A. `print preg_replace('/img=(\w+)/', '<img src="\1">', $text);`

   B. `print preg_replace('/img=(\S+)/', '<img src="\1">', $text);`

   C. `print preg_replace('/img=(\s+)/', '<img src="\1">', $text);`

   D. `print preg_replace('/img=(\w)+/', '<img src="\1">', $text);`

Answer **B** is correct. The characters / and . are not matched by \w (which only matches alphanumerics and underscores), or by \s (which only matches white-space).

3. Which of the following functions is most efficient for substituting fixed patterns in strings?

   A. preg_replace()

   B. str_replace()

   C. str_ireplace()

   D. substr_replace()

Answer **B** is correct. The PHP efficiency mantra is "do no more work than necessary." Both str_ireplace() and preg_replace() have more expensive (and flexible) matching logic, so you should only use them when your problem requires it. substr_replace() requires you to know the offsets and lengths of the substrings you want to replace, and is not sufficient to handle the task at hand.

4. If

```
$time = 'Monday at 12:33 PM';
```

or

```
$time = 'Friday the 12th at 2:07 AM';
```

which code fragment outputs the hour (12 or 2, respectively)?

   A. preg_match('/\S(\d+):/', $time, $matches);

      print $matches[1];

   B. preg_match('/(\w+)\Sat\S(\d+):\d+/', $time, $matches);

      print $matches[2];

   C. preg_match('/\s([a-zA-Z]+)\s(\w+)\s(\d+):\d+/', $time, $matches);

      print $matches[3];

   D. preg_match('/\s(\d+)/', $time, $matches);

      print $matches[1];

   E. preg_match('/\w+\s(\d+):\d+/', $time, $matches);

      print $matches[1];

Answer **E** is correct. Answer A and B both fail because \S matches nonwhitespace characters, which break the match. Answer C will correctly match the first $time correctly, but fail on the second because '12th' will not match [a-zA-Z]. Answer D matches the first, but will fail on the second, capturing the date (12) instead of the hour.

5. Which of the following output `True`?

   A. `if("true") { print "True"; }`

   B. `$string = "true";`

      `if($string == 0) { print "True"; }`

   C. `$string = "true";`

      `if(strncasecmp($string, "Trudeau", 4)) { print "True"; }`

   D. `if(strpos("truelove", "true")) { print "True"; }`

   E. `if(strstr("truelove", "true")) { print "True"; }`

Answers **A, B, C,** and **E** are correct. Answer A is correct because a non–empty string will evaluate to `true` inside an `if()` block. Answer B is covered in the chapter—when comparing a string and an integer with `==`, PHP will convert the string into an integer. `true` converts to `0`, as it has no numeric parts. In answer C, `strncasecmp()` returns `1` because the first four characters of 'Trud' come before the first four characters of `true` when sorted not case sensitively. Answer D is incorrect because `strpos()` returns `0` here (`true` matches `truelove` at offset 0). We could make this return `True` by requiring `strpos()` to be `!== false`. Answer E is correct because `strstr()` will return the entire string, which will evaluate to `true` in the `if()` block.

6

File Manipulation

Techniques You'll Need to Master

- How to open a file
- How to read from a file
- How to write to a file
- How to close a file
- How to interact with the filesystem
- How to lock files
- Miscellaneous functions for handling files

Terms You'll Need to Understand

- File resources
- File properties
- Advisory locking
- End of File

Interacting with files is a constant aspect of programming. Whether they are cache files, data files, or configuration files, the ability to manipulate files and their contents is a core skill for PHP programmers. In this chapter, you will learn how to open file stream resources for reading from and writing to files, as well as filesystem-level functions for manipulating file attributes.

Opening Files

When interacting with files in PHP, the first step is to open them. Opening files creates a resource that you must pass to the functions for reading, writing, and locking files. To open a file, use the `fopen()` function.

`fopen()` takes as its first parameter the filename to open, and as its second the *mode* with which to open the file. The filename can be either a local file or any network protocol that PHP understands. In this chapter, we will only discuss local files: Network streams will be covered in Chapter 10, "Stream and Network Programming." The mode determines what you can do with the file (read/write, write-only, read-only), where your file resource will start from (the beginning of the file or the end of the file), and what to do if the file does not exist (create it or fail). The complete list of modes is presented in Table 6.1. `fopen()` also takes an optional argument: a Boolean flag indicating whether the `include_path` should be searched (defaults to `false`).

Table 6.1 `fopen()` **Modes**

Mode	Description
r	Opens file for reading only; position is beginning of the file.
r+	Opens for reading and writing; position is beginning of the file.
w	Opens for writing only; position is beginning of the file; if the file does not exist, creates it.
w+	Opens file for reading and writing; position is beginning of the file; if the file does not exist, creates it.
a	Opens file for writing only; position is end of the file; if the file does not exist, creates it.
a+	Opens file for reading and writing; position is end of the file; if the file does not exist, creates it.
x	Creates and opens a file for writing; position is at the beginning of the file; if the file already exists, fails.
x+	Creates and opens a file for reading and writing; position is at the beginning of the file; if the file already exists, fails.

On Windows systems, you can also specify explicitly whether your file consists of binary or text data. (The default is text.) To do this, you can append a `b` or `t` to the mode, respectively. Failure to do this can result in writing corrupted binary files. Although this flag is only necessary on Windows platforms, it is recommended that you always use it for portability reasons.

If the `fopen()` call fails for any reason, it will return `false` and emit an `E_WARNING` level error; otherwise, it will return a stream resource for the file. For example, to open a file for appending information, you would use code such as this:

```
if(($fp = fopen($filename, "a")) === false) {
  // call failed, do something appropriate
}
// call succeeded, proceed normally
```

A call to fopen() can fail for a number of reasons—for example, if a file to be opened for reading does not exist or the executing user does not have sufficient permissions to open it with the specified mode.

Closing Files

After you are done accessing a file resource, you should close it. Unclosed files will be automatically closed by PHP at the end of a request. But if two processes write to the same file at the same time, they risk corruption, so you need to either close your files as expediently as possible or implement a locking scheme. To close an open file resource, you can use the fclose() function.

Reading from a File

When you have a valid file resource opened for reading, you can read from it in a number of ways. Before you go about performing reads, however, you should ensure that your stream resource still has data available. You can check this using the function feof(). feof() returns true if the file resource has hit *EOF (End Of File)*.

The most basic of the read functions is fread(). fread() takes as its two parameters the file resource handle to read from and the length to be read. It returns a string with the data that was read or false if an error occurred.

Here is an example of reading a file 1024 bytes at a time until it is complete:

```
if(($fp = fopen($filename, "r")) === false) {
  return;
}
while(!feof($fp)) {
  $buffer = fread($fp, 1024);
  // process $buffer
}
```

If you want to read your file resource a single line at a time, you can use the fgets() function. fgets() takes a file resource as its first argument and reads up to 1024 bytes from the file, returning when it reaches a newline. To change the maximum readable string length, you can pass a length as an optional second parameter. On success, the line just read (including its newline) is returned. If an error occurs, false is returned.

As an example, here is a code block that reads in a file of lines such as

```
foo=bar
```

and constructs an array using them as key value pairs:

```
$arr = array();
if(($fp = fopen($filename, "r")) === false) {
  return;
}
while(!feof($fp)) {
  $line = fgets($fp);
  list($k, $v) = explode('=', rtrim($line));
  $arr[$k] = $v;
}
```

The fpassthru() function allows you to directly output all the remaining data on a file resource. The following code checks the first four bytes of a file to see if it is a JPEG; if so, it sets the file resource position back to the start of the file using fseek() and outputs the entire file:

```
function output_jpeg($filename)
{
 if(($fp = fopen($filename, "rb")) === false) {
   return;
 }
 $line = fread($fp, 4);
 // check the 'magic number' of the file
 if($line === "\377\330\377\340") {
   fseek($fp, 0);
   fpassthru($fp);
 }
 fclose($fp);
}
```

Writing to a File

If you have a file resource opened for writing, you can write to it using fwrite(), which is the inverse of fread().

fwrite() takes as its first argument a file resource and as its second the string to write to that file. Optionally, you can pass a third argument—the maximum length that you want to write with the call. fwrite() returns the number of bytes written to the file resource. fputs() is an alias of fwrite()—they perform the exact same functions.

You can force a flush of all output to a file using the fflush() function. Flushing data is implicitly done when a file resource is closed, but is useful if other processes might be accessing the file while you have it open.

Here is an example of a function that appends time stamped data to a logfile:

```
function append_to_log($logline)
{
  if(($fh = fopen('debug.log', 'a')) === false) {
    die("Can not open debug.log");
  }
  fwrite($fh, time()." ".$logline."\n");
  fclose($fh);
}
```

Determining Information About Files

To get information about a file, you can use one of two sets of functions, depending on whether you have an open file resource for that file. If you do have a file resource, you can use the fstat() function. Calling fstat() on a file resource will return an array with the following keys:

"dev"	The device number on which the file lies
"ino"	The inode number for the file
"mode"	The file's mode
"nlink"	The number of hard links to the file
"uid"	The userid of the files owner
"gid"	The groupid for the file
"rdev"	The device type (if it's an inode device on UNIX)
"size"	The size of the file in bytes
"atime"	The UNIX time stamp of the last access of the file
"mtime"	The UNIX time stamp of the last modification of the file
"ctime"	The UNIX time stamp of the last change of the file (identical to mtime on most systems)
"blksize"	The blocksize of the filesystem (not supported on all systems)
"blocks"	The number of filesystem blocks allocated for the file

If you do not have an open file resource for a file, you can generate this same array using stat(), which takes the filename instead of the file resource. If the file does not exist, or if you do not have permissions to access the directories in the path to file, stat() will return false.

PHP also provides a number of 'shortcut' functions for accessing these individual properties. These functions are listed in Table 6.2. All these functions take the file's name as their sole argument.

Table 6.2 **File Property Convenience Function**

Function Name	Description
file_exists()	Returns true if the file exists
fileatime()	Returns the last access time of the file
filectime()	Returns the last change time of the file
filemtime()	Returns the last modification time of the file
filegroup()	Returns the file's groupid
fileinode()	Returns the file's inode
fileowner()	Returns the file's owner's uid
fileperms()	Returns the file's mode
filesize()	Returns the file's size in bytes
filetype()	Returns the type of file (inode, directory, fifo, and so on)
is_dir()	Returns true if the file is a directory
is_executable()	Returns true if the file is executable
is_file()	Returns true if the file is a regular file
is_link()	Returns true if the file is a soft link
is_readable()	Returns true if the file is readable
is_uploaded_file()	Returns true if the file was just uploaded via a HTTP POST request
is_writable()	Returns true if the file is writable

In addition to finding general information about files, these functions are useful for preventative error checking. For example, here is code that checks whether a file is readable and of nonzero length before opening it:

```
if(!is_file($filename) ||
   !is_readable($filename) ||
   !filesize($filename)) {
  die("$filename is not good for reading");
}
if(($fp = fopen($filename, "r")) === false) {
  die("Opening $filename failed")
}
```

Manipulating Files on the Filesystem

PHP also allows you to manipulate files: copying them, deleting them, changing their permissions, and more.

Copying, Deleting, and Moving Files

To copy a file, you can use the copy() function, which works as follows:

```
copy($source_file, $destination_file);
```

To delete a file, use the `unlink()` function:

```
unlink($filename);
```

To move a file, you can use `rename()`, which works like this:

```
rename($old_filename, $new_filename);
```

If the source and destination paths are on the same filesystem, `rename()` is *atomic*, meaning that it happens instantly. If the source and destination paths are on different filesystems, `rename()` must internally copy the old file to the new file and then remove the old file, which can take significant time for large files.

Changing Ownership and Permissions

To change the ownership of a file, you can use the `chown()` function. `chown()` takes the target filename as its first argument and either a username or userid as its second argument. Only the superuser can change the owner of a file, so you will likely only use this script in an administrative shell script.

To change the group of a file, you use the `chgrp()` function. `chgrp()` takes the target filename as its first parameter and the new groupname or groupid as its second parameter. Only the owner of a file can change its group, and then can only change it to a new group that the owner is also a member of.

To change the mode of a file, you use `chmod()`. The first argument is the target filename, and the second argument is the new mode in octal. It is important that the mode be an octal number and not a decimal number. Using a decimal number will not throw an error, but it will be internally converted into an octal number, most likely not resulting in what you intended.

Locking Files

To avoid the possibility of corruption when dealing with multiple processes writing to the same file, you can use locks to moderate access. PHP supports locking through the `flock()` function. The `flock()`-based locking function is discretionary, meaning that other `flock()` users will correctly see the locks, but if a process does not actively check the locks, that process can access the file freely. This means that your use of `flock()` needs to be consistent and comprehensive in order for it to be effective.

To use `flock()`, you first need to have an open file resource for the file you want to lock. You can then call `flock()` with that resource as its first argument, a locking operation constant as the second argument. The possible operations are

`LOCK_SH`	Try to acquire a shared lock
`LOCK_EX`	Try to acquire an exclusive lock
`LOCK_UN`	Release any locks

By default, these operations are all blocking. This means that if you try to take an exclusive lock while another process has a shared lock, your process will simply block, or wait, until the shared lock is released and the exclusive lock can be gained. Alternatively you can Boolean-OR the operation constant with LOCK_NB to have the operation fail if it would have blocked. If you use this nonblocking option, you can pass a third parameter that will be set to true if the call's failure was because the call would have blocked.

A typical use for locking is to safely append data to a file—for example, a logfile. This is composed of two functions: a writer and a reader. The writer takes an exclusive lock on the data file so that write access is serialized. The reader takes a shared lock so that it can read concurrently with other readers, but not conflict with writers. Here is code for the reader:

```
function retrieve_guestbook_data()
{
  if(($fp = fopen('guestbook.log', 'r')) === false) {
    die("Failed to open guestbook.log");
  }
  flock($fp, LOCK_SH);
  $data = fread($fp, filesize('guestbook.log'));
  flock($fp, LOCK_UN);
  fclose($fp);
  return $data;
}
```

Miscellaneous Shortcuts

In addition to the basic file functions, PHP offers a collection of 'shortcut' functions that allow you to handle common tasks with a single function call. In this final section, you will learn some of the more common shortcut functions available in PHP.

file()

Often you will want to convert a file into an array of its lines. The file() function performs this task. It takes the filename to read as its first argument and an optional flag as its second argument, specifying whether the include_path should be searched to find the file.

Because the entire file must be read in and parsed when file() is called, this function can be expensive if used on large files. For larger files, you will often want to open the file with fopen() and iterate over it line by line with fgets() to achieve a similar effect.

readfile()

Similar to fpassthru(), readfile() directly outputs an entire file. readfile ($filename) is equivalent to the following PHP code:

```
if($fp = fopen($filename, 'r')) {
  fpassthru($fp);
  fclose($fp);
}
```

file_get_contents()

Although it is possible to read an entire file into a string with the following code,

```
if(($fp = fopen($filename, "r")) === false) {
  $file = false;
} else {
  $file = fread($fp, filesize($filename));
}
fclose($fp);
```

it is much more efficient to use the built-in function file_get_contents(). That function will replace the entire previous loop with

```
$file = file_get_contents($filename);
```

Exam Prep Questions

1. What are the contents of output.txt after the following code snippet is run?

```
<?php
  $str = 'abcdefghijklmnop';
  $fp = fopen("output.txt", 'w');
  for($i=0; $i< 4; $i++) {
    fwrite($fp, $str, $i);
  }
?>
```

   A. abcd

   B. aababcabcd

   C. aababc

   D. aaaa

   The correct answer is **C**. On the first iteration, $i is 0, so no data is written. On the second iteration $i is 1, so a is written. On the third, ab is written, and on the fourth abc is written. Taken together, these are aababc.

2. Which of the following can be used to determine if a file is readable?

   A. stat()

   B. is_readable()

   C. filetype()

   D. fileowner()

   E. finfo()

The correct answers are **A** and **B**. stat() returns an array of information about a file, including who owns it and what its permission mode is. Together these are sufficient to tell if a file is readable. is_readable(), as the name implies, returns true if a file is readable.

3. Specifying the LOCK_NB flag to flock() instructs PHP to

   A. Return immediately if someone else is holding the lock.

   B. Block indefinitely until the lock is available.

   C. Block for a number of seconds dictated by the php.ini setting flock.max_wait or until the lock is available.

   D. Immediately take control of the lock from its current holder.

   The correct answer is **A**. The LOCK_NB flag instructs PHP to take a nonblocking lock, which immediately fails if another process holds the lock.

4. If you have an open file resource, you can read data from it one line at a time with the _____ function.

   The correct answer is fgets().

5. Which of the following functions require an open file resource?

   A. fgets()

   B. fopen()

   C. filemtime()

   D. rewind()

   E. reset()

   The correct answers are **A** and **D**. fgets() and rewind() both act on an open file resource. fopen() opens files to create resources, whereas filemtime() takes a filename and reset() acts on arrays.

7

Managing Dates and Times

Terms You'll Need to Understand

- UNIX time stamp
- UNIX epoch
- date arrays
- UTC
- Format strings

Techniques You'll Need to Master

- Handling dates in PHP
- Getting the current date
- Converting a string into a date
- Formatting dates and times

In this chapter, you will learn how to parse and manipulate dates and times in PHP. Handling dates and times is an important day-to-day skill for many PHP programmers. You will learn how to generate times from various date formats and multiple ways of formatting dates in strings.

How PHP Handles Dates

In PHP, you deal with dates and times in three basic formats:

- UNIX time stamps
- Date arrays
- String-formatted dates

Internally, PHP uses *UNIX time stamps*, which are the standard method of telling time on UNIX systems. UNIX time stamps tell the number of seconds that have passed since the *UNIX epoch*, which is defined as 00:00:00 January 1, 1970 in Coordinated Universal Time (abbreviated *UTC*). UTC was originally referred to as Greenwich Mean Time (or *GMT*), and the use of GMT is still common in colloquial usage (for example, in time zone names and in PHP function names).

> **Note**
>
> Coordinated Universal Time is abbreviated UTC because the French and English representatives to the standardization board could not agree to use the English (CUT) or French (TUC) abbreviations for the term and thus agreed on UTC as a compromise.

The current UNIX time stamp at the writing of this text is 1086455857, which corresponds to June 5, 2004 13:17:37 eastern daylight time.

As PHP's internal date format, UNIX time stamps are the common meeting ground for all the PHP date and time functions in that they all either take time stamps and render them into other formats, or take other formats and render them into time stamps. Because UNIX time stamps are integers, the various PHP date functions are only guaranteed to handle dates between 1970 and January 19, 2038 (corresponding with the maximum value of a signed 32-bit integer; on 64-bit systems this range is extended effectively indefinitely).

A more human-readable format that PHP can easily convert into its internal format is *date arrays*. A date array is an array consisting of the elements shown in Table 7.1.

Table 7.1 **Elements in a Date Array**

Key	Value
seconds	Number of seconds (0–59)
minutes	Number of minutes (0–59)
hours	Number of hours (0–23)
mday	Day of the month (1–31)
mon	Month of the year (1–12)
year	Year
wday	Day of the week (0–6)
yday	Day of the year (0–366)
weekday	Text representation of the day of the week (Sunday–Saturday)
month	Text representation of the month (January–December)

Additionally, PHP supports writing (and to a limited extent, reading) arbitrarily formatted date strings. Formatted date strings are most commonly used for presentation, but are clumsy for internal storage as they are more difficult to sort, manipulate, and parse than both UNIX time stamps and date arrays.

Getting the Current Time Stamp

The simplest way to get the current UNIX time stamp in PHP is to call the function `time()`, which returns the current UNIX time stamp. Here is an example that prints out its value:

```
print "The current UNIX time stamp is ".time();
```

If seconds-only granularity is not enough precision, you can use the `gettimeofday()` function. `gettimeofday()` returns an array consisting of the following key-value pairs:

sec	The current UNIX time stamp
usec	The number of microseconds past sec
minuteswest	The number of minutes offset from UTC ('west' of Greenwich)
dst	A flag to denote if it is currently daylight savings time

The microsecond information in `gettimeofday()` is useful for adding profiling information to code. An example follows:

```
function get_timer()
{
  $tm = gettimeofday();
  return $tm['sec'] + ($tm['usec']/1000000);
}

$start = get_timer();
sleep(1);
$finish = get_timer();

print "sleep(1) took ".($finish - $start)." seconds.";
```

Getting a Date Array

To get a date array, you can use the `getdate()` function. The `getdate()` function takes a UNIX time stamp as its first parameter and returns the date array for that time stamp in your current time zone (not UTC). If you don't pass any arguments to `getdate()`, it will return the date array for the current time. Here's an example that outputs the whole date array for the current time:

```
$now = getdate();
print_r($now);
```

This outputs

```
Array
(
    [seconds] => 37
    [minutes] => 23
```

```
    [hours] => 16
    [mday] => 5
    [wday] => 6
    [mon] => 6
    [year] => 2004
    [yday] => 156
    [weekday] => Saturday
    [month] => June
    [0] => 1086467017
)
```

Notice that the UNIX time stamp corresponding to the date returned is stored in index 0.

Optionally, you can use the `localtime()` function that mimics the C function of the same name. `localtime()` is almost identical to `getdate()` with a few important differences:

- By default, the date array that is returned is indexed and not associative.
- The month returned is in the range 0–11, where January is 0.
- The year is returned as the year since 1900. Thus 2004 is represented as 104.

Like `getdate()`, if you call `localtime()` with no arguments, it will return information for the current time. You can also pass `localtime()` a UNIX time stamp, and it will return you the date array for that. For example, to get the date array for now

```
$now = localtime();
```

Running this right now (on Saturday, June 5, 2004), `$now` is set to:

```
Array
(
    [0] => 30  // seconds
    [1] => 53  // minutes
    [2] => 15  // hours
    [3] => 5   // day of the month
    [4] => 5   // month of the year (0-11, NOT 1-12)
    [5] => 104 // years since 1900
    [6] => 5   // day of the week
    [7] => 155 // day of the year
    [8] => 1   // daylight savings time flag
)
```

Alternatively, you can set a second optional parameter to 1 to have the array returned to you as an associative array. Here is an example of how to extract the date array for exactly one day ago as an associative array:

```
$yesterday = localtime(time() - 24*60*60, 1);
```

Now $yesterday is set to the following:

```
Array
(
    [tm_sec] => 19
    [tm_min] => 1
    [tm_hour] => 16
    [tm_mday] => 4
    [tm_mon] => 5
    [tm_year] => 104
    [tm_wday] => 5
    [tm_yday] => 155
    [tm_isdst] => 1
)
```

Formatting a Date String

To create a formatted date string from a UNIX time stamp, PHP provides two families of functions—date() and strftime(). Both perform the same basic operation, but differ in the formatting tokens that they use.

The first of these functions is date(). date() takes a format string and a UNIX time stamp and fills out the format accordingly. If the time stamp is omitted, the current time is used. The formatting tokens available to date() are summarized in Table 7.2.

Table 7.2   date() **Formatting Tokens**

Character	Description
a	Lowercase am/pm
A	Uppercase AM/PM
d	Day of the month (01–31)
D	Three letter day abbreviation (Sun–Sat)
F	Name of the month (January–December)
g	Hour, 12-hour format without leading zeros (1–12)
G	Hour, 24-hour format without leading zeros (0–23)
h	Hour, 12-hour format with leading zeros (01–12)
H	Hour, 24-hour format with leading zeros (00–23)
i	Minutes with leading zeros (00–59)
j	Day of the month without leading zeros (1–31)
I	1 if date is daylight savings time, else 0
l	Full text day of the week (Sunday–Saturday)
L	1 if current year is a leap year, else 0
m	Number of the month with leading zeros (01–12)
M	Three letter month abbreviation (Jan–Dec)

Table 7.2 **Continued**

Character	Description
n	Number of the month without leading zeros (1–12)
O	UTC offset in hours (–1200–+1200)
r	RFC 2822 formatted date
s	Seconds, with leading zeros (00–59)
S	English ordinal counting suffix for day of the month(st, nd, rd, and so on)
t	Number of days in the current month
T	Time zone (EST, PST, and so on)
U	UNIX time stamp
w	Day of the week (0–6)
W	ISO-8601 week number of the year (1–52)
Y	Year, 4-digit format (2004, and so on)
z	Day of the year (0–365)
Z	UTC offset in seconds (–43200–+43200)

The following code will print the line 'The time is now 6:05 PM' (or whatever the current time is when you run it):

```
print "The time is now ".date('g:i A');
```

When assembling a date string, any character that is not a recognized formatting token will be printed as is. To print a literal character that is a formatting character, you need to escape it in the format string with a backslash. For example, an ISO-8601 date string looks like the following:

```
2004-06-05T18:05:01-0500
```

To print this out with date, your format string will look like this:

```
$iso8601 = date('Y-m-d\TH:i:sO');
```

Notice that the dashes and colons are represented literally, but the 'T,' which is also a formatting character, needs to be escaped.

date() always formats its output relative to your machine's time zone. To format dates in UTC, you can use the gmdate() function. To see the difference, compare the output of

```
print "The local ISO-8601 date string is ". date('Y-m-d\TH:i:sO');
```

and

```
print "The UTC ISO-8601 date string is ". gmdate('Y-m-d\TH:i:sO');
```

When I run both fragments at 6:05 p.m. eastern standard time, the first code outputs the following:

```
The local ISO-8601 date string is 2004-06-05T18:05:01-0500
```

whereas the second outputs this:

```
The UTC ISO-8601 date string is 2004-06-05T23:05:01+0000
```

The date() function can handle most date formatting needs, but suffers from two problems:

- The use of literal characters as tokens makes complicated formatting a bit cumbersome, as you have to escape most everything in the format.
- All the textual names returned are in English.

To remedy this problem, you can use the strftime() function, which works exactly like date() except that it has its own formatting token set (from the C function strftime) and all of its textual names are derived from your locale settings. On most systems, the locale is the standard 'C' locale, but you can also set it to a multitude of regional preferences.

The formatting tokens available to strftime() are listed in Table 7.3.

Table 7.3 strftime() **Formatting Tokens**

token	description
%a	Short day name (Sun–Sat in the C locale)
%A	Full day name (Sunday–Saturday in the C locale)
%b	Short month name (Jan–Dec in the C locale)
%B	Full month name (January–December in the C locale)
%c	The preferred date and time representation in the current locale
%C	Century number
%d	Day of the month with zeros padded (01–31)
%D	A shortcut for %m/%d/%y
%e	Day of the month without zeros padded (1–31)
%g	The 2-digit year corresponding to the ISO-8601 week number for the given day (see %V)
%G	The 4-digit year corresponding to the ISO-8601 week number for the given day (see %V)
%h	Short month name (Jan–Dec in the C locale)
%H	Hour, 24-hour format with leading zeros (00–23)
%I	Hour, 12-hour format with leading zeros (01–12)
%j	Day of the year with leading zeros (001–366)
%m	Month with leading zeros (01–12)
%M	Minute with leading zeros (00–59)
%n	A newline (\n)
%p	Ante meridian/post meridian (a.m./p.m. in C locale)
%r	Time in a.m./p.m. format (equivalent to %I:%M:%S %p in the C locale)
%R	Time in 24-hour format (equivalent to %H:%M in the C locale)

Table 7.3 **Continued**

token	description
%s	The UNIX time stamp
%S	Second with leading zeros (00–59)
%t	A tab (\t)
%T	Same as %H:%M:%S
%u	The day of the week as an integer, (1—7, where 1 is Monday)
%U	Week number of the current year as an integer (00–53, starting with the first Sunday as week 01)
%V	The ISO 8601 week number of the current year, (01–53, where week 1 is the first week that has at least four days in the current year and a Monday as the first day of the week.)
%W	The week number of the current year as an integer (00–53 with the first Monday as the first day of week 01)
%x	The locale-preferred representation of just the date
%X	The locale-preferred representation of just the time
%y	Year in two-digit format (04, and so on)
%Y	The year including the century (2004, and so on)
%z	The UTC offset in hours (-1200–+1200)
%Z	The time zone abbreviation
%%	A literal % character

Because the strftime() formatting tokens use % to mark the start of a token, it is easy to include literal text in the format string. Here is some code that demonstrates both the use of literal text in a format string and locale-specific formatting:

```
$locale = setlocale(LC_TIME, NULL);
echo strftime("The current day in the $locale locale is %A\n");
// Set locale to 'French'
$locale = setlocale(LC_TIME, "fr_FR");
echo strftime("The current day in the $locale locale is %A\n");
```

Starting with default locale settings, this outputs

```
The current day in the C locale is Saturday
The current day in the fr_FR locale is Samedi
```

Similar to date(), strftime() takes a UNIX time stamp to use as its second parameter—if it is not passed, the current time is used. Here is a code block that prints the abbreviated names of the next seven days:

```
for($i=0;$i<7;$i++) {
  print strftime("%a\n", time() + $i*24*60*60);
}
```

Also similar to `date()`, `strftime()` has a version that will print times in the UTC time zone: `gmstrftime()`.

Getting a UNIX Time Stamp from a Date Array

To get the UNIX time stamp for a date represented by a date array, you can use the `mktime()` function. `mktime()` takes the following arguments (all optional):

```
mktime([int hour [, int minute [,int sec [, int month [, int day
➥ [, int year [, int dst]]]]]]]);
```

If any of the values are omitted, the appropriate values from the current time are used.

To find the UNIX time stamp for New Year's 2000 in your time zone, you would use the following line:

```
$newyears_ts = mktime(0, 0, 0, 1, 1, 2000);
```

On my system (eastern standard time), `$newyears_ts` equals `946702800`.

To find out the UNIX time stamp for 3 p.m. today, you can use

```
$ts = mktime(15, 0, 0);
```

The unspecified fields (month, day, year) will default to the current day.

To get the UNIX time stamp for a UTC date array, you can use the `gmmktime()` function. Here is the code to get the UNIX time stamp for New Year's 2000 in Greenwich, England (UTC +0000):

```
$newyears_ts = gmmktime(0, 0, 0, 1, 1, 2000);
```

Getting a UNIX Time Stamp from a String

The most complex PHP date function is `strtotime()`, which takes an arbitrarily formatted date string and attempts to parse it into a UNIX time stamp. `strtotime()` supports both absolute time formats such as `'October 10, 1973'`, as well as relative time formats such as `'next Tuesday 10am'`. `strtotime()` uses the same date-parsing engine as the GNU system utility tar, so any date format supported there is supported by `strtotime()` as well.

Here is an example of using `strtotime()` to get the UNIX time stamp of today at six o'clock:

```
$ts = strtotime("Today 6 pm");
```

or, alternatively

```
$ts = strtotime("Today 18:00");
```

`strtotime()` can be cleverly confusing, though. If instead of `"Today 6 pm"` you had used `"Today at 6 pm"`, your time stamp would not be correct. This is because `strtotime()` interprets `"at"` as the time zone for the Azores and adjusts the time stamp accordingly.

Also, certain time formats can befuddle `strtotime()`. For example, this code will cause $ts to be set to -1, indicating an error:

```
$ts = strtotime("Fri, 9 Jan 2004 03:26:23 +0000 GMT");
```

`strtotime()` has become confused because two separate time zone offsets (+0000 and GMT) were both specified. If you are manually constructing all the inputs to `strtotime()` (for example, to take advantage of the `next week`/`last week` functionality) this is not an issue, as you can test your inputs to make sure that they are all correctly handled. However, if you are using `strtotime()` to handle arbitrarily formatted date entries (for example, submitted free form through a web page), you should take into account the possibility of both incomprehensible and improperly interpreted dates.

One of the best aspects of `strtotime()` is using it to handle leap years and daylight saving time. If you need to find the time stamp for the current time tomorrow, you cannot simply look 24 hours in the future, as it might be 23 or 25 hours if you cross a daylight saving time boundary. `strtotime()` takes this into account, though; so to find a this time tomorrow, you could just say

```
$tomorrow = strtotime("tomorrow")
```

Because you did not specify a time, `strtotime()` uses the current value.

Exam Prep Questions

1. Which of the following sentences are incorrect?

   A. `date()` returns the current UNIX datestamp.

   B. `date()` returns a formatted date string.

   C. `date()` requires a time stamp to be passed to it.

   D. `date()` returns a date array.

   The correct answers are **A**, **C**, and **D**. `date()` takes a format string and an optional time stamp and produces a formatted date string. If a UNIX time stamp is not passed into `date()`, it will use the current time.

2. The _____ function will return the current UNIX time stamp.

   The correct answer is `time()`.

3. Which of the following functions will output the current time as `11:26 pm`?

   A. print date('H:m a');

   B. print date('G:M a');

   C. print date('G:i a');

   D. print strftime('%I:%M %p');

   The correct answers are **C** and **D**.

4. The PHP date functions are only guaranteed to work for dates after _____.

   A. January 1, 1970 00:00:00

   B. January 1, 1900 00:00:00

   C. January 1, 1963 00:00:00

   D. January 18, 2038 22:14:07

The correct answer is **A**. The UNIX epoch is January 1, 1970 00:00:00 UTC. On 32-bit systems, the date functions are only guaranteed to work until January 19, 2038.

5. Internally PHP handles dates and times as

   A. A 'date array' array consisting of the year, month, day, hour, minute, and second.

   B. A UNIX time stamp representing the number of seconds since the UNIX epoch.

   C. An ISO-8601 date entity.

   D. A UNIX time stamp consisting of the number of microseconds since the UNIX epoch.

The correct answer is **B**. PHP stores all its dates internally as UNIX time stamps, which are defined as the number of seconds since the UNIX epoch, January 1, 1970 00:00:00 UTC.

8

Managing Email

Introduction

Terms You'll Need to Understand

- sendmail wrapper
- SMTP
- Headers
- MIME encoding
- SMTP (Windows only)
- smtp_port (Windows only)
- sendmail_from (Windows only)
- sendmail_path

Techniques You'll Need to Master

- Mail functions
- URL functions

How Email Is Delivered

If you are going to be writing and deploying PHP scripts that generate and send email messages, you need to know something about how email gets delivered around the Internet. This will help you better understand and support your customers when problems arise. Figure 8.1 shows the main components of the email architecture.

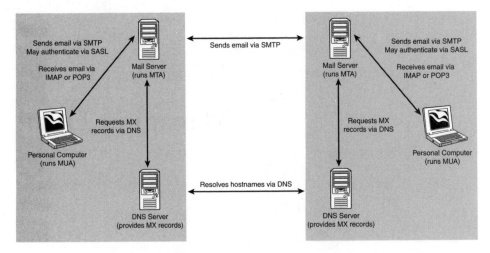

Figure 8.1   How email is delivered.

Here are the standard terms that you will come across at some point or another.

MTA—Mail Transport Agent

When email is sent from organization to organization, it is sent from email server to email server. The software that runs on your email server and handles sending and receiving email from around the Internet is called the *Mail Transport Agent* (*MTA* for short). Examples of Mail Transport Agents are

- sendmail
- postfix
- qmail
- Microsoft Exchange
- Lotus Notes

Mail transport agents talk to each other using the SMTP network protocol.

SMTP—Simple Mail Transport Protocol

The *Simple Mail Transport Protocol (SMTP)* is the standard network-layer protocol for transmitting an email message across the Internet.

Servers normally listen for incoming SMTP connections on port 25.

MX Records

When an MTA has an email message to send to another MTA, it has to convert the address in the To:, Cc:, or Bcc: line into an IP address. Everything after the @ sign in the address is taken to be the *email domain*. This is normally something such as @php.net.

The email domain isn't the real name of a server. It looks like a real name (and has to follow the same rules), but it isn't. It's actually a special kind of DNS alias.

To receive email for your email domain, you have to add an MX record for that email domain to your DNS server.

> **Note**
>
> If you don't set up an MX record in your DNS server, the MTA will look for a matching A record instead.

MUA—Mail User Agent

The *Mail User Agent (MUA)* is the jargon name for an email client.

Examples of Mail User Agents are

- Outlook Express
- Evolution
- KMail
- pine
- mutt
- Hotmail

A PHP script that sends email is also a type of Mail User Agent.

Mail User Agents read email directly from files on disk, via network protocols such as POP3 or IMAP, or via proprietary network protocols (as used by Microsoft Exchange).

Mail User Agents normally send their email by connecting to a Mail Transport Agent over the network via the SMTP network protocol. Some UNIX-based Mail User Agents might send their email instead by executing a *sendmail wrapper* program.

When a Mail User Agent connects to an MTA via SMTP to send email, it might use SASL to authenticate the user.

SASL—Simple Authentication and Security Layer

The *Simple Authentication and Security Layer (SASL)* is a tried and trusted way to bolt user-authentication onto existing network protocols. SMTP has been extended (via the SMTP AUTH command) to support SASL.

If an MTA has been configured to require authentication, only MUAs with built-in support for the SMTP AUTH command will be able to connect to send email.

Other Emerging Technologies

Although email is as old as the Internet itself, the rise of unsolicited bulk email (commonly called *spam*), the increasing number of modern viruses that transmit themselves via email, and the fraudulent use of genuine email addresses for criminal intent mean that we are at the start of a period of great change in how email will be delivered in the future.

Junk email filters have become very popular. They can be added both to the MTA and/or the MUA. It's a fair bet that most of the email that these filters mark as 'junk' never gets read by a human. Junk email filters aren't perfect; genuine email that looks very like real junk email will also get marked as junk. When you roll out a PHP application that sends email, you should perform some tests with your customer to make sure that your email will get past whatever junk email filter your customer uses.

Because of repeated security holes in MUAs, the more tech-savvy businesses and users do not accept delivery of HTML email. It's very tempting to send HTML email—such emails look so much nicer than plain-text email. You should ensure that any PHP application you write that sends email always gives the user the option to choose between plain-text email and HTML email. You should never only support HTML email.

If you write and sell PHP software that works with email, it's important that you keep abreast of the new technologies that are always coming out. When capturing requirements from your customer, always make sure that you've agreed what email technologies the customer has adopted—or is planning to adopt within six months of the end of your project. The customer will (somewhat naively) expect your PHP application to work perfectly with whatever changes he plans to make to his email infrastructure—and will blame you if it doesn't.

Preparing PHP

Before you can send email from your PHP script, you must first ensure that your copy of PHP has been correctly configured.

If You Are Using PHP on UNIX

To send email from a PHP script running on UNIX, you must have a sendmail-compatible MTA installed on the same server that your PHP script runs on.

On UNIX systems, PHP sends email by running the command-line program sendmail. sendmail is the de facto standard MTA for UNIX systems.

If you are using an alternative to sendmail, it must provide a sendmail wrapper. A *sendmail wrapper* is a drop-in replacement for the sendmail command-line program. It must accept the -t and -i command-line switches at the very least.

When PHP is compiled, the configure script searches for the sendmail command in

```
/usr/bin:/usr/sbin:/usr/etc:/etc:/usr/ucblib:/usr/lib
```

If configure cannot find the sendmail command, then sendmail support will be permanently disabled. The following PHP functions will either be missing entirely, or will always return an error:

- mail()—will be missing
- ezmlm_hash()—will be missing
- mb_send_mail()—will always return false

When this happens, you must install a sendmail wrapper, and then recompile PHP. Once PHP is compiled with sendmail support enabled, whenever your script sends email, PHP will use the `sendmail` command discovered by the `configure` script. If you ever need to override this default, set the `sendmail_path` in `php.ini` to point to the `sendmail` command that you want PHP to use.

```
sendmail_path = '/usr/local/bin/sendmail'
```

If You Are Using PHP on Windows or Netware

Although not documented in the PHP Manual, if you set the `sendmail_path` setting in your `php.ini` file, PHP will attempt to send email via the sendmail_wrapper—behaving exactly as if PHP were running on UNIX. This can catch you out, so remember to look for it when troubleshooting email problems.

If you do not have a sendmail wrapper available, PHP on Windows talks to the mail transport agent (MTA) directly via the SMTP network protocol. PHP needs to be configured to tell it where to find your MTA:

- The `SMTP` setting in `php.ini` must be set to the hostname (or IP address) of the email server that your MTA is running on. The default value is `localhost`. You will probably want to change that.

- The `smtp_port` setting in `php.ini` must be set to the port that your MTA is listening on. The default value is `25`. You probably will not need to change that.

Note
It isn't documented in the PHP Manual, but PHP on Novell Netware uses the same code for email support as PHP on Windows.

Caution
It is currently not possible to get PHP on UNIX to talk directly to the MTA via SMTP.

PHP on Windows does not support SASL. If your MTA is configured to require authentication, you will need to change the security on your MTA to enable PHP to send emails through successfully.

On UNIX, the MTA will automatically say that the email is from whichever user your PHP script is running as.

This can't be done on Windows because PHP is connecting to the MTA over the network via SMTP. Instead, PHP will work out who the email is from by looking in these places in this order:

- the `from:` header line passed to the `mail()` function
- the `sendmail_from` setting in the `php.ini` file

PHP will display an error and refuse to send the email if it cannot determine who the email is from.

If you compile your own version of PHP on Windows, and you are going to use it to send emails, it's important that you build PHP with the Perl-compatible regular expression (PCRE) library included. PHP on Windows relies on the PCRE functions to make sure that headers have the correct end of line character. If you build PHP on Windows without PCRE support, you might find that MTAs refuse to accept your emails for delivery.

With PHP correctly configured, you can now send email from your PHP scripts.

Sending Email

Use the PHP function `mail()` to send an email message from a PHP script.

The first parameter of the `mail()` function is the email address to send the email message to.

Assuming that you are running your PHP script on the server that is the MTA for the example.com email domain, and that there is a local user called `fred`, all of these are valid email addresses:

- `fred`

    The MTA thinks you are trying to send an email to the local user `fred`.

- `fred@example.com`

    This is the normal form for an email address, and the one that you are probably most familiar with.

- `fred @ example.com`

    The MTA will automatically collapse the whitespace in the email address.

    Although perfectly legal, email addresses with whitespace are seldom seen today.

- `"Fred Bloggs" <fred@example.com>`

    The MTA will automatically extract the `fred@example.com` from between the angular brackets.

    The entire string will be added as is to the From: line of the email message.

    Note that the double quotes are important—do not leave them out.

Sending an Email to More Than One Recipient

Add additional addresses to the `to` parameter. Separate them by a comma and a space:

```
fred, joe@example.com, "Jane Doe" <jane.doe@example.com>
```

If you want to cc: or bcc: an email to someone, do this by adding additional headers to your email.

Managing Email Headers

Email headers are lines of text that go at the start of an email message. Headers hold information used by MTAs and MUAs. If you pass a list of additional headers into the `mail()` function, it will automatically add these headers to your email message. Each header in the list must be separated by `\r\n`.

The Cc: and Bcc: Headers

The Cc: and Bcc: headers allow you to send a copy of an email message to other people. All recipients will be able to see the list of addresses in the To: and Cc: lines of the email, but will not be able to see the list of addresses in the Bcc: line.

The Cc: and Bcc: headers are optional. If you provide either of them (or both of them), they must follow the same rules about email addresses as the `to` parameter to `mail()`.

The From: Header

The From: header tells the MTA who is sending the email message.

If you do not provide a From: header, PHP might or might not add one for you:

- If you are sending email via the sendmail wrapper, PHP will leave it to the MTA to add a default From: header.
- If you are sending email on Windows without using the sendmail wrapper, PHP will use the `sendmail_from` setting in `php.ini` to set a default From: header.

Setting the Subject

The second parameter to `mail()` is a string containing the "subject" of the email. Whatever you put in this string will appear in the Subject: header of the email.

Formatting an Email Message

The third parameter to `mail()` is the email message itself.

Plain-Text Emails

Plain-text emails are normal 7-bit US-ASCII strings with each line terminated by `\r\n`. The following code will send a plain-text email, as long as PHP is configured to correctly send email and the MTA is working, too.

> **Note**
>
> Some MTAs on UNIX will accept messages that just use `\n` as the end-of-line sequence. This is nonstandard behavior, and you should expect to have problems eventually.

```php
<?php

// who is the email going to?
// change this to be *your* email address ;-)

$to = "stuart";

// what is the message?

$message = "This is my first email message, sent from PHP.\r\n"
          . "This is a second line of text\r\n";

// who else do we want to send the message to?

$more_headers = "Cc: stuart\r\n";

// send the email

$result = mail (
        $to,
        "My first e-mail sent from PHP",
        $message,
        $more_headers
);

?>
```

By default, all emails sent via mail() are plain-text emails. If you want to send HTML emails, you need to create a simple MIME-encoded email.

Basic HTML Emails

The *Multipurpose Internet Mail Extensions (MIME)* define a standardized way of sending emails with attachments, and/or with content that isn't 7-bit US-ASCII.

You can find a reference to the MIME standard in the "Further Reading" section at the end of this chapter.

To send a basic HTML email, all you need to do is this:

- Add these additional headers:

  ```
  MIME-Version: 1.0
  Content-Type: text/html; charset="iso-8859-1"
  Content-Transfer-Encoding: 7bit
  ```

- Pass your HTML content in a string as the third parameter to mail().

Any images, links, stylesheets—anything at all that the web browser has to download—must be full URLs. Note that, for security and privacy reasons, most email clients will not automatically download anything that's referenced in an HTML email.

If you want to add images to your email, you need to use attachments.

Attaching a File to a Message

To attach a file to an email message, you have to create a multipart MIME message.

- Pass these headers as the fourth parameter to `mail()`:

```
MIME-Version: 1.0
Content-Type: multipart/mixed; boundary="php-12345"
```

Note the *boundary* on the end of the `Content-Type`. The boundary is an arbitrary US-ASCII string that tells MUAs when the end of a MIME block has been reached. You can set it to be whatever you want, provided you set it to something that isn't going to appear in your email message.

- The first part of your message string should be a plain text message like this:

```
If you are reading this, it means that your email client does not
support MIME.  Please upgrade your email client to one that sup-
ports MIME.
—php-12345
```

Note the boundary marker after the message. This tells MIME that you've reached the end of this particular part of the email message. You can now add more parts to your email message.

- The second part of your "message" string should be the message itself. You need to add `Content-Type` and `Content-Transfer-Encoding` headers to the message, followed by the message itself.

```
Content-Type: text/plain; charset="iso-8859-1"
Content-Transfer-Encoding: 7bit
Hello, this is my plain text message.  If you can see this, then
hopefully my MIME email is working fine.
—php-12345
```

Note the boundary marker after the message. You have to put the boundary marker at the end of each part of the message.

- Next come the attachments. Each attachment gets added to the "message" string as well. You need to add `Content-Type` and `Content-Transfer-Encoding` headers, and then the attachment.

If the attachment isn't plain text, you should encode it using base64 encoding:

```
Content-Type: image/jpeg
Content-Transfer-Encoding: base64
<message goes here>
```

```
    —php-12345

<?php

// who is the email going to?
// change this to be *your* email address ;-)

$to = "stuart";

// what is the message?

$message = "This is my third email sent from "
         . "<a href=\"http://www.php.net\">PHP</a>.\r\n"
         . "This email has an attached image\r\n";

// don't forget our blank line
$blank_line = "\r\n";

// define our boundary
$boundary_text = "php-12345";
$boundary = "—" . $boundary_text . "\r\n";
$last_boundary = "—" . $boundary_text . "—\r\n";

// add the MIME headers

$more_headers = "MIME-Version: 1.0\r\n"
              . "Content-Type: multipart/mixed; boundary=\""
              . $boundary_text
              . "\"\r\n";

// create the first part of the message
$mime_message = "If you are reading this, it means that your e-mail client\r\n"
              . "does not support MIME.  Please upgrade your e-mail client\r\n"
              . "to one that does support MIME.\r\n"
              . $boundary;

// add the second part of the message
$mime_message .= "Content-Type: text/html; charset=\"iso-8859-1\"\r\n"
              . "Content-Transfer-Encoding: 7bit\r\n"
              . $blank_line
              . $message
              . $boundary;
```

```
// now add the attachment
$mime_message .= "Content-Type: image/gif; name=\"php.gif\"\r\n"
            . "Content-Transfer-Encoding: base64\r\n"
            . "Content-disposition: attachment; file=\"php.gif\"\r\n"
            . $blank_line
            . chunk_split(base64_encode(file_get_contents("php.gif")))
            . "\r\n"
            . $last_boundary;

// send the email

$result = mail (
        $to,
        "My first HTML e-mail with an attachment",
        $mime_message,
        $more_headers
);

?>
```

You can add as many attachments as you want, but remember—they can make the email quite large to download, and many users are still using dial-up rather than broadband!

The last boundary marker in the email message must end with –. For example, if our boundary marker is

```
–php-12345
```

the last marker in the email message would be

```
–php-12345–
```

instead.

Attached Images for HTML Emails

HTML emails will attempt to download their images and stylesheets from your web server. Because of security and privacy reasons, many MUAs will refuse to attempt these downloads, ruining the look of your HTML email message.

You can add your images as attachments to your email, and then point your HTML at the attached images:

- Change the first Content-Type of your email to be multipart/related. Don't forget to include the boundary definition.

- When you add an image as an attachment, include this additional header:

  ```
  Content-Location: URL
  ```

  URL is the URL that you use inside the <img> tag to include your image.

```php
<?php

// who is the email going to?
// change this to be *your* email address ;-)

$to = "stuart";

// what is the URL of the image?

$image = http://static.php.net/www.php.net/images/php.gif;

// what is the message?

$message = "This is my fourth email sent from "
        . "<a href=\"http://www.php.net\">PHP</a>.\r\n"
        . "This email has an image "
        . "<img src=\""
        . $image
        . "\"> here.\r\n";

// don't forget our blank line
$blank_line = "\r\n";

// define our boundary

$boundary_text = "php-12345";
$boundary = "-" . $boundary_text . "\r\n";
$last_boundary = " . $boundary_text . "-\r\n";

// add the MIME headers

$more_headers = "MIME-Version: 1.0\r\n"
             . "Content-Type: multipart/related; boundary=\""
             . $boundary_text
             . "\"; type=\"text/html\"\r\n";

// create the first part of the message
$mime_message = "If you are reading this, it means that your e-mail client\r\n"
             . "does not support MIME.  Please upgrade your e-mail client\r\n"
             . "to one that does support MIME.\r\n"
             . $boundary;

// add the second part of the message
$mime_message .= "Content-Type: text/html; charset=\"iso-8859-1\"\r\n"
             . "Content-Transfer-Encoding: 7bit\r\n"
             . $blank_line
             . $message
             . $boundary;
```

```
// now add the attachment
$mime_message .= "Content-Type: image/gif; name=\"php.gif\"\r\n"
            . "Content-Transfer-Encoding: base64\r\n"
            . "Content-Location: "
            . $image
            . "\r\n"
            . $blank_line
            . chunk_split(base64_encode(file_get_contents("php.gif")))
            . "\r\n"
            . $last_boundary;

// send the email

$result = mail (
        $to,
        "My first HTML e-mail with an embedded image",
        $mime_message,
        $more_headers
);

?>
```

Using Extra Command-Line Parameters

The fifth argument to mail() is a list of parameters to use when executing the sendmail wrapper.

These parameters have no effect at all if you are using PHP on Windows without a sendmail wrapper.

A Word About Email Delivery

mail() returns TRUE if the email is accepted for delivery. This does not guarantee that the email will be delivered.

Internet email is an unguaranteed delivery system.

Email messages can be lost at any point between your MTA and your user's MUA. This is often caused by a catastrophic disk failure on an MTA, combined with inadequate backups. When email messages are lost, there is no automatic mechanism to trigger re-sending the email message. Lost email messages are never delivered to the intended recipient.

A more common problem is email messages that get rejected by the user's MTA. Causes include

- Inbox over quota
- Email too large to accept

- Disabled user account
- Misspelled email address name
- Virus scanner detected a virus in an attachment

When an MTA rejects an email message, it normally sends back the email message with a description of why the email was rejected. These 'bounced' email messages are never delivered to the intended recipient.

If the email message is successfully delivered to the intended recipient, this can still cause problems. The user might use a filter that bounces email from senders not in a whitelist. The user might have set up a vacation auto-responder, which automatically sends back a message saying that the user is currently out of the office.

It's therefore essential that your PHP application can cope with these situations:

- Every single email you send should have a valid Reply-To: header, to allow receipt of bounced email messages. You should set up a mailbox just for bounces to emails sent from your PHP scripts. It's a good idea to have someone go through the mailbox once a day, just in case there is anything you can do about the bounced email.

- Normally, there should be a way for the user of your PHP script to make your script send the email again.

- Any order confirmations, receipts, and invoices that you send via email should also be available through some other means—either via your website, or via snail mail. Apart from being good customer service, many of these documents are legally important.

Further Reading

The standards for email handling are defined by the RFC series of documents, which you can find at http://www.rfc-editor.org/.

- RFC's 821 and 822 are the current standards on SMTP and plain-text emails, respectively.
- RFC's 2045, 2046, 2047, 2048, and 2049 define the MIME standard.
- RFC 1896 discusses the "text/enriched" MIME content type. This is very similar—but not the same as—HTML email.
- RFC 2557 defines the use of Content-IDs to use attached images in HTML emails.
- RFC 2554 defines the use of SASL for authenticating connections to an MTA.
- Internet Mail Consortium home page http://www.imc.org/. In particular, http://www.imc.org/terms.html is an excellent reference.

Exam Prep Questions

1. Your company sells a shopping cart written in PHP. Matching common industry practice, the shopping cart sends a confirmational email to the user after he has checked out.

   Your team has just ported the shopping cart from PHP on Gentoo Linux to PHP running on Windows Server 2003. They've correctly set the SMTP, smtp_port, and sendmail_from settings in php.ini, but this error appears when the shopping cart tries to send the confirmation email:

   ```
   Could not execute mail delivery program 'sendmail'
   ```

   This is your team's first project using Windows Server, and everyone's a bit confused as to why this error is happening. The php.ini settings work fine on Linux, so what could be the problem?

   Choose from one of the following:

   A. The smtpserver service hasn't been started.

   B. sendmail_path in php.ini needs to be commented out.

   C. Microsoft Exchange needs configuring to accept email from PHP.

   D. PHP cannot send email when running on Windows.

   The correct answer is **B**.

2. Flush with the success of the shopping cart on Windows Server 2003, your company has decided that it would be a good idea to add Solaris to the list of supported operating systems. Because the shopping cart is already proven to work on Linux, it should be no trouble at all to get the cart working on Solaris.

   Your team goes out and buys a new Sun server. As Solaris doesn't come with PHP, you have to compile PHP by hand. At the same time, your network administrator decides to un-install the Solaris version of sendmail and replace it with the company's standard MTA—postfix—instead. He forgets to tell you that he's done this.

   When the time comes to test your shopping cart on Solaris, there's a problem. When the shopping cart tries to send the confirmation email, you get this error message:

   ```
   Call to undefined function: mail()
   ```

   What can you do to fix this problem?

   A. Put an @ symbol in front of your call to mail() so that PHP does not output the error message.

   B. Put sendmail back on the machine. Postfix doesn't provide a sendmail wrapper anyway.

    C. Use `mb_send_mail()` instead.

    D. Recompile PHP—after asking your network administrator to leave the MTA alone until the recompilation of PHP has completed

The correct answer is **D**.

3. All the new customers you're attracting on Solaris are very pleased with your shopping cart. Your product is earning them a lot of new customers also.

    However, like all customers, they want new features. Specifically, they want you to create and attach a simple comma-separated file that users can import into products such as Microsoft Money. This will make it easier for customers to manage their finances. Besides, it's a cool feature that none of your competitors have, so the marketing department has told your boss to get it done.

    At the moment, the shopping cart sends out RFC-822–compliant plain-text emails. What do you need to change to make it send the attachment as well?

    Choose from one of the following:

    A. Replace your plain-text emails with MIME-encoded emails.

    B. Refuse to do it. RFC-822 doesn't allow attachments, and your company should not be shipping products that go against Internet standards.

    C. Put the CSV file on a web server, and put a link to it in the email.

    D. Ditch PHP's built-in `mail()` function, and use the `system()` command to call sendmail directly.

The correct answer is **A**.

4. A rival has just launched a new version of his shopping cart. Unlike yours—which only sends plain-text emails—his shopping cart sends out confirmation emails that look more like a web page. These emails look so much nicer, and he's starting to eat into your sales as a result. It's a good thing his cart only runs on Windows; otherwise, you'd have no customers left!

    Something must be done, and marketing has decided that if you can't beat them, join them. Your long-suffering boss has been told to make your shopping cart send out nice-looking emails too. In the best tradition of pointy-haired bosses, he's dumped the whole problem in your lap, and is waiting for you to tell him how this can be done.

    What could you do to make this work? Choose one or more of the following:

    A. Change your emails to send `text/html` MIME-encoded emails.

    B. It's time to ditch `mail()` again and call sendmail directly.

    C. Change your emails to send `text/enriched` MIME-encoded emails.

    D. Tell your boss that this only works on Windows because PHP on Windows handles emails very differently.

The correct answers are **A** and **C**.

5. During testing of your new, much nicer-looking confirmation emails, you notice that there's a problem. The email uses quite a few images—including the all-important company logo. All of these images are stored on your web server, and the email uses standard "`<img src=...>`" tags to include them. The images look great in your email client—but appear as missing images when you send the email to your boss to show him the results of your hard work.

    Your boss isn't pleased, and neither is the marketing department, who make it very clear that you can't ship the code until the company logo shows up.

    The good news is that it isn't just your email. The confirmation emails sent by your rival also have this problem. If you can figure out how to make it work, not only will you be playing catch-up to your rival, but you'll also be back in the lead. This mollifies your boss, but gets you nowhere nearer to solving the problem.

    What could you change to make this work? Choose one or more of the following:

    A. `sendmail` is too old. Replace it with a modern MTA instead.

    B. Add all the images to the email as attachments with `Content-Locations`, and make your email use the attachments rather than the images on the website.

    C. Add a piece of inline JavaScript in your email that temporarily changes the security settings of the email client. This will enable the images to be downloaded.

    D. File a bug with the author of the email client that your boss uses. Something must be wrong with the way it handles RFC-1896–compliant email messages.

    The correct answer is **B**—and only **B**.

6. With all the problems overcome, your company's shopping cart now sends email messages that not only look great, but also work where your rival's do not. Marketing is pleased, and has awarded your boss a bonus in return. Isn't that typical?

    However, the support team leader isn't happy. Since the release of your latest shopping cart marvel, there has been a large increase of bug reports about your new style email messages. It seems that many users won't accept HTML emails at all, and would like to be able to send plain-text emails instead.

    Seeing as he just got a nice bonus for adding HTML emails, your boss isn't too sympathetic to the idea of getting rid of them again. In desperation, the support team leader turns to you, and asks you to convince your boss.

    Draft out a short email message to your boss, explaining why plain-text emails are a good idea. As all consultants need to be politicians at heart, it might help to think about how you can keep both your boss and the support team leader happy.

9

PHP and Databases

PHP IS USED TOGETHER WITH A DATABASE SERVER (DBMS) of some kind, and the platform (of which the DBMS is part) is usually referred to by an acronym that incorporates a particular brand of database—for example, LAMP stands for Linux/Apache/MySQL/PHP.

When it comes to the certification program, however, you are not required to know how *any* DBMS in particular works. This is because, in a real-world scenario, you might find yourself in a situation in which any number of different DBMSs could be used. Because the goal of the certification program is to test your proficiency in PHP—and not in a particular DBMS—you will find yourself facing questions that deal with the best practices that a PHP developer should, in general, know about database programming.

This doesn't mean that you shouldn't expect technical, to-the-point questions—they will just be less based on actual PHP code than on concepts and general knowledge. You should, nonetheless, expect questions that deal with the basic aspects of the SQL language in a way that is DBMS agnostic—and, if you're used to a particular DBMS, this might present a bit of a problem because the SQL language is quite limited in its nature and each specific DBMS uses its own dialect that is often not compatible with other database systems.

As a result, if you are familiar with databases, you will find this chapter somewhat limited in its explanation of database concepts and techniques because we are somewhat constrained by the rules set in place by the certification process. However, you can find a very large number of excellent resources on creating good databases and managing them, both dedicated to a specific DBMS and to general techniques. Our goal in this chapter is to provide you with the basic elements that you are likely to find in your exam.

Terms You'll Need to Understand

- Database
- Table
- Column
- Key
- Index
- Primary key
- Foreign key
- Referential Integrity
- Sorting
- Grouping
- Aggregate functions
- Transaction
- Escaping

Techniques You'll Need to Master

- Creating tables
- Designing and optimizing indices
- Inserting and deleting data
- Selecting data from tables
- Sorting resultsets
- Grouping and aggregating data
- Using transactions
- Escaping user input
- Managing dates

"Databasics"

Most modern general-purpose DBMSs belong to a family known as "relational databases." In a relational DBMS, the information is organized in *schemas* (or databases), which, in turn contain zero or more *tables*. A table, as its name implies, is a container of *rows* (or records)—each one of which is composed of one or more columns (or fields).

Generally speaking, each column in a table has a data type—for example, integer or floating-point number, variable-length character string (VARCHAR), fixed-length character string (CHAR), and so on. Although they are not part of the SQL-92 standard, many databases define other data types that can come in very handy, such as large text strings, binary strings, and sets. You can expect pretty much every DBMS to implement the same basic types, so most of the time you won't have much of a problem porting data from one to the other as needed.

Indices

Databases are really good at organizing data, but they need to be instructed as to *how* the data is going to be accessed.

Imagine a situation in which you have a table that contains a million telephone numbers and you want to retrieve a particular one. Because the database doesn't normally know how you're going to access the data, its only choice will be to start at the beginning of the table and read every row until it finds the one you requested.

Even for a fast computer, this could be a very costly proposition in terms of performance, particularly if the telephone number you're looking for is at the end of the list.

To solve this problem, database systems introduce the concept of "index." Just like the index on your telephone directory, indices in a database table enable the server to optimize the data stored in the table so that it can be retrieved quickly and efficiently.

Writing Good Indices

As you can imagine, good indexing is possibly one of most crucial aspects of a fast and efficient database. No matter how fast your database server is, poor indexing will always undermine your performance. What's worse, you won't notice that your indices are not working properly until enough data is in a table to make an impact on your server's capability to retrieve information quickly in a sequential way, so you might end up having bottlenecks that are not easy to solve in a situation in which there is a lot of pressure on you to solve them rapidly.

In an ideal situation, you will be working side-by-side with a database administrator (DBA), who will know the ins and outs of your server and help you optimize your indices in a way that best covers your needs. However, even without a DBA on hand, there are a few rules that should help you create better indices:

- Whenever you write a query that accesses data, try to ensure that your table's indices are going to be able to satisfy your selection criteria. For example, if your search is limited by the contents of columns A, B, and C, all three of them should be part of a single index for maximum performance.

- Don't assume that a query is optimized just because it runs quickly. In reality, it might be fast only because there is a small amount of data and, even though no indices are being used, the database server can go through the existing information without noticeable performance deterioration.

- Do your homework. Most DMBSs provide a set of tools that can be used to monitor the server's activity. These often include the ability to view how each query is being optimized by the server. Spotting potential performance issues is easy when the DBMS itself is telling you that it can't find an index that satisfies your needs!

Primary Keys

The columns that are part of an index are called *keys*. A special type of index uses a key known as a "primary key." The primary key is a designated column (or a set of columns) inside a table whose values must always respect these constraints:

- The value assigned to the key column (or columns) in any one row must not be NULL.
- The value assigned to the key column (or columns) in any one row must be completely unique within the table.

Primary keys are extremely important whenever you need to uniquely identify a particular row through a single set of columns. Because the database server automatically enforces the uniqueness of the information inserted in a primary key, you can take advantage of this fact to ensure that you don't have any duplicates in your database. For example, if the user "John Smith" tries to create an account in your system, you can designate the user's name as the primary key of a table to ensure that he can't create more than one account because the DBMS won't let you create two records with the same key.

In some database systems, the primary key also dictates the way in which records are arranged physically by the data storage mechanism that the DBMS used. However, this does not necessarily mean that a primary key is more efficient than any other properly designed index—it simply serves a different purpose.

Foreign Keys and Relations

A staple of relational databases is the concept of "foreign key." A foreign key is a column in a table that references a column in another table. For example, if you have a table with all the phone numbers and names of your clients, and another table with their addresses, you can add a column to the second table called "phone number" and make it a foreign key to the phone number in the first table. This will cause the database server to only accept telephone numbers for insertion in the second table if they also appear in the first one.

Foreign keys are extremely important because they can be used to enforce *referential integrity*—that is, the assurance that the information between tables that are related to each other is self-consistent. In the preceding example, by making the phone number in the second table a foreign key to the first, you ensure that the second table will never contain an address for a client whose telephone number doesn't exist in the first.

Even though the SQL standard does require the ability to define and use foreign keys, not all popular DBMSs actually implement them. Notably, MySQL versions up to 5.0 have no support for this feature.

Even if your database system doesn't support relational integrity, you can still support it within your applications—in fact, you will have to anyway because you will have to advise your users appropriately when they make a mistake that would cause duplicate or orphaned records to be created.

Creating Tables or Adding and Removing Rows

Although the exact details of the syntax used to create a new table varies significantly from one DBMS to another, this operation is always performed by using the CREATE TABLE statement, which usually takes this form:

```
CREATE TABLE table_name
(
  Column1 datatype[,
  Column2 datatype[,
  ...]]
)
```

It's important to note that a table must have at least one field because its existence would be completely meaningless otherwise. Most database systems also implement limits on the length of each field's name, as well as the number of fields that can be stored in any given table (remember that this limit can be circumvented, at least to a certain degree, by creating multiple tables and referencing them using foreign keys).

Inserting a Row

The INSERT statement is used to insert a new row inside a table:

```
INSERT [INTO] table_name
[(column1[, column2[, column]])]
VALUES
(value1[, value2[, valuen]])
```

As you can see, you can specify a list of columns in which you are actually placing data, followed by the keyword VALUES and then by a list of the values you want to use. Any column that you don't specify in your insertion list is automatically initialized by the DBMS according to the rules you defined when you created the table. If you don't specify a list of columns, on the other hand, you will have to provide a value for each column in the table.

Deleting Rows

The DELETE statement is used to remove one or more rows from a table. In its most basic form, it only needs to know where the data is being deleted from:

```
DELETE [FROM] table_name
```

This command deleted all the rows from a particular table. Normally, this is not something that you will actually want to do during the course of your day-to-day operations—almost all the time, you will want to have a finer degree of control over what is deleted.

This can be accomplished by specifying a WHERE clause together with your DELETE statement. For example,

```
DELETE FROM my_table
WHERE user_name = 'Daniel'
```

This will cause all the rows of my_table, in which the value of the user_name column is 'Daniel', to be deleted. Naturally, a FROM clause can contain a wide-ranging number of different expressions you can use to determine which information is deleted from a table with a very fine level of detail—but those go beyond the scope of this chapter. Although a few basic conditions are common to most database systems, a vast number of these implement their own custom extensions to the WHERE syntax.

Retrieving Information from a Database

The basic tool for retrieving information from a database is the SELECT statement:

```
Select *
From my_table
```

This is perhaps the most basic type of data selection that you can perform. It extracts all the values for all the columns from the table called my_table. The asterisk indicates that we want the data from all the columns, whereas the FROM clause indicates which table we want to extract the data from.

Extracting all the columns from a table is, generally speaking, not advisable—even if you need to use all of them in your scripts. This is because by using the wildcard operator, you are betting on the fact that the structure of the database will never change—someone could remove one of the columns from the table and you would never find out because this query would still work.

A better approach consists of explicitly requesting that a particular set of values be returned:

```
Select column_a, column_b
From my_table
```

As you can see, you can specify a list of columns by separating them with a comma. Just as with the DELETE statement, you can narrow down the number of rows returned by using a WHERE clause. For example,

```
Select column_a, column_b
From my_table
Where column_a > 10 and column_b <> 'Daniel'
```

Extracting Data from More Than One Table

One of the most useful aspects of database development is the fact that you can spread your data across multiple tables and then retrieve the information from any combination of them at the same time using a process known as *joining*.

When joining multiple tables together, it is important to establish how they are related to each other so that the database system can determine how to organize the data in the proper way.

The most common type of join is called an *inner join*. It works by returning the rows from two tables in which a common key expression is satisfied by both tables. Here's an example:

```
Select *
From table1 inner join table2 on table1.id = table2.id
```

When executing this query, the database will look at the `table1.id = table2.id` condition and only return those rows from both tables where it is satisfied. You might think that by changing the condition to `table1.id <> table2.id`, you could find all the rows that appear in one table but not the other. In fact, this causes the DBMS to actually go through each row of the first table and extract all the rows from the second table where the `id` column doesn't have the same value, and then do so for the second row, and so forth—and you'll end up with a resultset that contains every row in both tables many times over.

You can, on the other hand, select all the rows from one of the two tables and only those of the other that match a given condition using an *outer join*. For example,

```
Select *
From table1 left outer join table2 on table1.id = table2.id
```

This will cause the database system to retrieve all the rows from `table1` and only those from `table2` where the `id` column has the same value as its counterpart in `table1`. You could also use `RIGHT OUTER JOIN` to take all the rows from `table2` and only those from `table1` that have the `id` column in common.

Because join clauses can be nested, you can create a query that selects data from an arbitrary number of tables, although some database systems will still impose a limitation on the number of columns that you can retrieve.

Aggregate Functions

The rows of a resultset can be grouped by an arbitrary set of rows so that aggregate data can be determined on their values.

The grouping is performed by specifying a `GROUP BY` clause in your query:

```
SELECT *
From my_table
Group by column_a
```

This results in the information extracted from the table to be grouped according to the value of `column_a`—all the rows in which the column has the same value will be placed next to each other in the resultset.

You can now perform a set of operations on the rows known as *aggregates*. For example, you can create a resultset that contains the sum of all the values for one column grouped by another:

```
Select sum(column_b)
From my_table
Group by column_a
```

The resultset will contain one row for each value of `column_a` with the sum of `column_b` for all the rows in `my_table` that contain that value.

A number of different aggregate functions can be used in your queries. The most popular are

- `AVG()`—Calculates the mean average value of all the values for a specific column
- `COUNT()`—Calculates the number of rows that belong to each grouping
- `MIN()` and `MAX()`—Calculate the minimum and maximum value that appears in all the rows for a specific column.

It's important to remember that, in standard SQL, whenever a GROUP BY clause is present in a query, only fields that are either part of the grouping clause or used in an aggregate function can be selected as part of the query. This is necessary because multiple values exist for every other column for any given row in the resultset so that the database server couldn't really return any one of them arbitrarily.

This limitation notwithstanding, some DBMSs (notably MySQL) actually allow you to include columns in your query that are neither part of the grouping clause nor encapsulated in an aggregate function. This can come in very handy under two very specific circumstances: when all the values for a particular column are the same for every value of the grouping clause (in which case the column could be a part of the grouping clause itself) or when you *really* know what you're doing.

In general, however, the certification program deals with standard SQL, where this syntax is not allowed. Also, remember that the GROUP BY clause is not, in itself, an aggregate function.

Sorting

One of the great strengths of databases is the ability to sort the information they retrieve from their data stores in any number of ways. This is accomplished by using the ORDER BY clause:

```
Select *
From my_table
Order by column_a, column_b DESC
```

This query retrieves all the values from `my_table`, and then sorts them by the value of `column_a` in ascending order. Any rows in which the value of `column_a` is the same are further sorted by the value of `column_b` in descending order (as determined by the `DESC` clause).

Sorting is very powerful, but can have a significant impact on your database's performance if the indices are not set up properly. Whenever you intend to use sorting clauses, you should carefully analyze your queries and ensure that they are properly optimized.

Transactions

When more than one operation that affects the data contained in a schema is performed as part of a larger operation, the failure of every one of them can wreak havoc on your data's integrity. For example, think of a bank that must update your account information—stored in a table that contains your actual financial operations and another one in which your account balance is stored—after a deposit. If the operation that inserts the information about the deposit is successful but the update of your balance fails, the table in which your account data is stored will contain conflicting information that is not easy to highlight by using the DBMS's built-in functionality.

This is where transactions come into place: They make it possible to encapsulate an arbitrary number of SQL operations into a single atomic unit that can be undone at any time until it is finally committed to the database.

The syntax for creating transactions—as well as support for them—varies with the type of DBMS used, but generally speaking, it works like so:

```
BEGIN TRANSACTION
(Your data-altering instructions here)
[COMMIT TRANSACTION | ROLLBACK TRANSACTION]
```

If the `COMMIT_TRANSACTION` command is issued at the end of a transaction, the changes made by all the operations it contains will be applied to the database. If, on the other hand, `ROLLBACK TRANSACTION` is executed instead, all the changes are discarded.

Transactions are useful in a number of situations and, despite their name, their usefulness is not limited to the financial world—generally speaking, whenever you need to perform a set of operations that must all be successful in order for the data to maintain its integrity.

PHP and Databases

When it comes to interfacing a PHP script to a database, there is one golden rule: *never trust user input*. Of course, this rule should apply to any aspect of your scripts. But when dealing with databases, it is paramount you ensure that the data that reaches the database server is pristine and has been cleared of all possible impurities.

Thus, you must ensure that the data coming from the user is properly *escaped* so that it cannot be interpreted by the database server in a way you're not expecting. For example, consider this little script:

```php
<?php

$connection = database_connect ('server', 'user', 'password');

database_exec ($connection, "Insert my_table Values ('{$_POST['username']}'")");

?>
```

If the user passes this input as the value of the username POST variable, you'll be in trouble:

```
'); Delete my_table; select ('
```

When inserted in the query, the following will actually be executed:

```
Insert my_table Values (''); Delete my_table; select();
```

This results in the deletion of every row in my_table—probably not what you had in mind.

PHP provides an escaping mechanism for most DBMSs—you need a different one because each database platform defines its own escaping rules. For example, if you're using MySQL, you can use the mysql_escape_string() function for the purpose.

There's Date and *Date*

Another problem that typically affects PHP's interoperation with databases is the fact that dates are stored and manipulated in very different ways by the two environments.

As you saw in Chapter 7, "Managing Dates and Time," PHP's date functionality relies on the UNIX timestamp, which has some severe limitations, particularly in its resolution below the second and in the range of dates that it can represent.

Most databases use an extended date format capable of representing a wide range of dates that goes well beyond the timestamp's capabilities. When accessing a database, you must keep this problem in mind and provide your own mechanism for handling dates.

Exam Prep Questions

1. Which of the following is not an aggregate function?

    A. AVG

    B. SUM

    C. COUNT

    D. GROUP BY

    E. MIN

    The correct answer is **D**. Group by is a grouping clause, not an aggregate function.

2. In the following query, how will the resultset be sorted?

```
Select * from my_table order by column_a desc, column_b, column_c
```

    A. By `column_a` in descending order, by `column_b` in descending order, and, finally, by `column_c`.

    B. By `column_a`, `column_b`, and `column_c`, all in descending order.

    C. By `column_a`, `column_b`, and `column_c`, all in ascending order.

    D. By `column_a`. Any rows in which `column_b` has the same value will then be resorted by `column_c` in descending order.

    E. By `column_a` in descending order. Any rows in which `column_a` has the same value will then be ordered by `column_b` in ascending order. Any rows in which both `column_a` and `column_b` have the same value will be further sorted by `column_c` in ascending order.

E is the correct answer. The resultset of the query will, first of all, be sorted by the value of `column_a` in descending order, as dictated by the DESC clause. If, after the first sorting operation, any rows have the same value for `column_a`, they will be further sorted by `column_b` in ascending order. If any rows have the same value for `column_a` and `column_b`, they will be further sorted by `column_c` in ascending order.

3. How is a transaction terminated so that the changes made during its course are discarded?

    A. ROLLBACK TRANSACTION

    B. COMMIT TRANSACTION

    C. By terminating the connection without completing the transaction

    D. UNDO TRANSACTION

    E. DISCARD CHANGES

A and **C** are both valid answers. A transaction is not completed when the connection between your script and the database server is discarded, as if a ROLLBACK TRANSACTION command has been issued.

10

Stream and Network Programming

Terms You'll Need to Understand

- File wrappers
- Streams
- Sockets
- Blocking calls

Techniques You'll Need to Master

- Filesystem functions
- Network functions
- Socket functions
- Stream functions
- URL functions
- List of supported protocols/wrappers
- List of supported transports

`php.ini` Settings to Understand

- `allow_url_fopen` (Filesystem)
- `auto_detect_line_endings` (Filesystem)
- `default_socket_timeout` (Filesystem)
- `from` (Filesystem)
- `user_agent` (Filesystem)

What Are File Wrappers?

File wrappers are pieces of code that PHP uses to read from and write to different types of files. They are part of PHP's Streams architecture.

File wrappers allow you to use PHP's built-in filesystem functions on things that aren't normal files.

Figure 10.1 shows what happens when you access a file. When your PHP script needs to work with a file, you use one of the filesystem functions that PHP provides. These file system functions hand the work off to the file wrappers. PHP chooses the correct file wrapper based on the name of the file. The file wrapper does the work and passes the results back through PHP to your script.

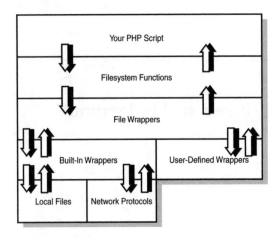

Figure 10.1   Accessing a file in PHP.

PHP comes with a number of built-in file wrappers. Additionally, you can create file wrappers of your own using the PHP Streams API.

How Do You Choose Which File Wrapper Is Used?

You tell PHP which file wrapper to use by passing URLs to the filesystem functions that accept filenames. URLs look like this:

```
scheme://path/to/file
```

or like this:

```
\\smbserver\share\path\to\file
```

If you do not supply a scheme, PHP will automatically assume that you are trying to work with a traditional disk-based file.

```php
<?php

// Chapter 10: Stream And Network Programming
//
// Example 01: Selecting a file wrapper using fopen()

// we will open the this example script file
//
// this uses the file:// wrapper

echo "This file is called:" . __FILE__ . "\n";
$fp = fopen(__FILE__, "r");
fclose($fp);

?>
```

What Built-In Wrappers Does PHP Provide?

PHP comes with a number of file wrappers that you can use.

- `file://`

  This file wrapper allows you to work with traditional local files.

- `\\smbserver\share\path\to\file`

  This file wrapper allows you to access files using Microsoft's file sharing or a compatible UNIX solution such as Samba.

- `http://` and `https://`

  This file wrapper allows you to communicate with a website using the HTTP network protocol. This file wrapper only supports retrieving data from a website.

  Use the user_agent setting in `php.ini` to tell the remote web server what type of browser you want content for. Many sites use the user agent string to send back content tailored to the capabilities of the web browser.

- `ftp://` and `ftps://`

  This file wrapper allows you to communicate with FTP servers. You can use this wrapper to download files from the FTP server and to upload files to the FTP server.

  When logging in to an FTP server as the anonymous user, it is etiquette to use your email address as the password. Set the from setting in `php.ini` to your email address, and the FTP wrapper will automatically do this for you.

- `php://`

  This file wrapper gives you access to PHP's standard input, output, and error streams. The main use of this file wrapper is to read raw HTTP POST data.

- compression streams—`compress.zlib://` and `compress.bzip2://`

  This file wrapper allows you to read files that have been compressed using the gzip (`.gz` files) or bzip2 (`.bz2` files), respectively. You can also use this wrapper to create compressed files too.

You can also create your own file wrappers in PHP and register them using the `stream_wrapper_register()` function in PHP 4.3.2 and later.

Not All Wrappers Are Created Equal

There are ten low-level operations that wrappers support. It's not possible to make every wrapper support every one of these operations. When working with a wrapper, check to see which of these operations are supported. Look in the "List of Supported Wrappers/Protocols" appendix in the PHP Manual for this information.

- Restricted by `allow_url_fopen`

  The `allow_url_fopen` setting in the `php.ini` file can be used to prevent scripts from accessing files across the network.

  Some file wrappers are affected by this setting, and some file wrappers are not. Check the file wrapper you want to use to see.

- Allows reading

  This operation allows you to read data using the file wrapper.

  Most built-in file wrappers support this operation. The main ones that don't are `php://stdout` and `php://stderr`.

- Allows writing

  This operation allows you to write data using the file wrapper.

  Some built-in file wrappers support this operation, and some do not. An example of a file wrapper that does not support this operation is the `http://` file wrapper.

- Allows appending

  This operation allows you to add data to the end of whatever it is you are accessing.

  An example of a file wrapper that supports this operation is the `compress.zlib://` wrapper. An example of a file wrapper that does not support this operation is the `ftp://` wrapper.

- Allows simultaneous reading and writing

  This operation allows you to open a single file for both reading and writing at the same time.

  Most built-in file wrappers do not support this operation.

  Even if the file wrapper does not allow you to open a file for both reading and writing, the file wrapper might allow you to open a file just for reading or just for writing. A good example of this is the FTP file wrapper. Using this file wrapper, you can FTP files to a remote server (you can write to the file), and you can FTP files from a remote server (you can read from the file), but it is impossible to FTP the file to the remote server and to FTP the file from the remote server at the same time.

- Supports `stat()`

  The `stat()` function provides information about the file.

  Some file wrappers allow you to access things or data that you normally cannot obtain, or that do not contain data to start with.

- Supports `unlink()`

  The `unlink()` function allows you to delete the file.

  Some file wrappers allow you to access things that you cannot delete. These file wrappers therefore cannot support the `unlink()` function.

- Supports `rename()`

  The `rename()` function allows you to change the name of the file.

  Some file wrappers allow you to access things that you cannot rename. These file wrappers therefore cannot support of the `rename()` function.

- Supports `mkdir()`

  The `mkdir()` function allows you to create a directory (also known as a folder on Windows).

  Some file wrappers allow you to access things that do not support directories. Other file wrappers allow you to access things that do not let you create new directories. These wrappers therefore cannot support the `mkdir()` function.

- Supports `rmdir()`

  The `rmdir()` function allows you to delete a directory or folder.

  Some file wrappers allow you to access things that do not support directories. Other file wrappers allow you to access things that do not let you delete directories. These wrappers therefore cannot support the `rmdir()` function.

Using a File Wrapper

When you have selected a file wrapper using `fopen()`, you can use the file handle that `fopen()` returns with the following filesystem functions:

- `fclose()`
- `feof()`
- `fflush()`
- `fgetc()`
- `fgetcsv()`
- `fgets()`
- `fgetss()`
- `flock()`
- `fpassthru()`
- `fputs()`

- `fread()`
- `fscanf()`
- `fseek()`
- `fstat()`
- `ftell()`
- `ftruncate()`
- `fwrite()`
- `rewind()`
- `set_file_buffer()`

Depending on the file wrapper you are using, some of these functions might return an error. For example, you cannot use `fwrite()` with the `http` file wrapper because the `http` file wrapper only supports reading and not writing.

Correctly Detecting Line Endings

The Windows, UNIX (and UNIX-like systems such as Linux), and Apple Macintosh (Mac OS) operating systems all use a different sequence of characters to denote the end of a line of text.

The `fgets()` function retrieves a complete line of text from a stream by looking for the end-of-line characters in the stream. By default, `fgets()` looks for a default sequence of characters and makes no attempt to determine which operating system the file came from.

The `auto_detect_line_endings` setting in the `php.ini` file allows you to change the behavior of `fgets()`. Set this setting to `on` to tell `fgets()` to determine the correct end-of-line character sequence by reading the file, instead of using the default sequence.

Closing a File Wrapper

When you have finished with your file, it is good practice to close the file handle by using `fclose()`.

PHP will close the file handle for you when your script terminates if you haven't already done so. However, there is an operating-system–enforced limit to the number of files that PHP can have open at once. You can ensure that you never hit this limit by closing your file handles as soon as you are done with them.

Other Functions That Work with File Wrappers

In PHP 4.3.0 and later, there are a number of functions that can be used with file wrappers to work with (possibly remote) files:

- `copy()`
- `file_get_contents()`
- `file()`
- `readfile()`

Support for file wrappers will be added to many more functions in PHP 5.

Introducing Streams

Streams are the way that PHP handles access to and from files and network services. Whenever you use file wrappers—whenever you are accessing a file—PHP automatically creates a stream for you in the background. Figure 10.2 shows what a stream looks like.

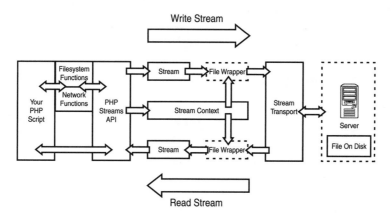

Figure 10.2   The PHP streams architecture.

Streams are made up from a number of smaller components. Each stream has a transport, perhaps a file wrapper, one or two pipelines, and perhaps a context. PHP also maintains metadata about the stream.

What Is Stream Metadata?

Stream metadata is data about the stream itself. It tells you

- what components the stream has been made from
- additional data in the file wrapper that you cannot get at using `fread()` and others
- the amount of data available for your PHP script to read

- whether the stream connection has timed out or not
- whether the stream has blocked or not
- whether all data has been read from the stream or not

To get stream metadata, use the `stream_get_meta_data()` function.

```php
<?php

// Chapter 10: Stream and Network Programming
//
// Example 02: stream metdata example

// we will create a stream by opening this stream, and then we'll
// dump the metadata out to see what's there

echo "Metadata for file: " . __FILE__ . "\n\n";

$fp = fopen(__FILE__, "r");
var_dump(stream_get_meta_data($fp));
fclose($fp);


?>
```

Here is the output from running the code example:

```
array(6) {
  ["wrapper_type"]=>
  string(9) "plainfile"
  ["stream_type"]=>
  string(5) "STDIO"
  ["unread_bytes"]=>
  int(0)
  ["timed_out"]=>
  bool(false)
  ["blocked"]=>
  bool(true)
  ["eof"]=>
  bool(false)
}
```

```php
<?php

// Chapter 10: Stream and Network Programming
//
// Example 03: stream metadata example - http file wrapper

// we will create a stream by opening a connection to the PHP Project's
// own web server, and then dump the metadata to see what we have
```

```
echo "Metadata from a connection to: http://www.php.net/\n\n";

$fp = fopen("http://www.php.net/", "r");
stream_filter_append($fp, "string.rot13");
var_dump(stream_get_meta_data($fp));

fclose($fp);

?>
```

Pipelines

Data in a stream flows along one of two pipelines:

- Data sent down a stream from your PHP script to the destination file or network server flows down the write pipeline.
- Data retrieved from the file or network server flows up the read pipeline.

Some streams will have both pipelines, but some streams will only have a read pipeline or a write pipeline.

What Is the Stream Transport?

At the far end of the pipeline, the furthest away from your PHP script, is the stream transport. The stream transport is a piece of code that enables the file wrapper to talk directly with whatever the stream is connected to.

PHP comes with a number of built-in transports:

- STDIO

    The STDIO transport is used to talk to normal files, special resources such as stdin and stdout, and any other types of file supported by your underlying operating system.

- socket

    The socket transport is used to talk to (possibly remote) servers over the network.

PHP automatically chooses the correct transport to use with your choice of file wrapper.

What Is the Stream Context?

The stream context is a piece of data about the stream and about the data passing along the stream. It is used to pass additional options to the file wrapper or stream transport.

You create the context using the stream_context_create() function, and then pass it as a parameter to fopen() or fsockopen().

Different file wrappers and stream transports accept different options. You can pass options to both the file wrapper and underlying stream transport at the same time.

How Do Streams Affect Me?

Most of the time, you will be using streams via `fopen()` and the file wrappers. PHP always manages the stream for you, and you can pay it little mind under these circumstances.

If you have to directly interact with the stream, it will probably be to pass options through to the file wrapper via a stream context, or to retrieve extra information from the file wrapper via the stream's metadata.

The other time that you will need to work more closely with the stream is if you are writing PHP code to talk over the network to remote servers and services using network protocols.

Connecting to Remote Hosts Using Sockets

When you access a normal file, all file operations ultimately are handled by your computer's operating system. The operating system creates a resource called a file handle. File handles make it easy for the operating system to understand which file PHP is reading from or writing to.

When you access a (possibly remote) server over the network, all the operations on this connection are also handled by your computer's operating system. Instead of creating a file handle, the operating system creates a resource called a socket. File handles and sockets are very similar, and through the PHP Streams architecture, PHP tries to keep the differences to a minimum.

When Should I Use a Socket Instead of a File Wrapper?

Some file wrappers allow you to access (possibly remote) network servers. For example, the `http` file wrapper allows you to retrieve pages from a web server. Unlike sockets, file wrappers will hide the details of supporting the application-layer network protocol.

So why would you want to use a socket instead?

You must use a socket if you want to connect to a (possibly remote) network server that there is no file wrapper for. An example would be connecting to the memcached caching server. There is no file wrapper that supports the memcached network protocol.

You must use a socket if you want to do something that the file wrapper cannot do—but is possible through the underlying network protocol. An example would be sending an XML-RPC message to a (possibly remote) web server. XML-RPC involves sending XML messages to and from the web server, using the HTTP network protocol. The `http` file wrapper only supports reading from a web server; it does allow you to write data to the web server. But the underlying HTTP network protocol does support writing data to a web server, and you can access this network protocol by using a socket rather than by using a file wrapper.

What Network Transports Does PHP Support?

You can find this information in the "List of Supported Socket Transports" appendix in the PHP Manual.

- `tcp`

  This transport allows you to connect to (possibly remote) network servers using the connection-orientated Transmission Control Protocol—the TCP part of TCP/IP.

- `udp`

  This transport allows you to connect to (possibly remote) network servers using the connection-less User Datagram Protocol—part of the TCP/IP network protocol.

- `ssl`

  This transport allows you to connect to (possibly remote) network servers using Secure Sockets Layer encryption. SSL runs over TCP connections.

- `tls`

  This transport allows you to connect to (possibly remote) network servers using Transport Layer Security encryption. TLS runs over TCP connections.

- `unix`

  This transport allows you to connect to services running on the local computer using the connection-orientated UNIX Domain protocol.

- `udg`

  This transport allows you to connect to services running on the local computer using the connection-less UNIX Domain protocol.

How Do I Open a Socket?

You can create a socket using the `fsockopen()` and `pfsockopen()` functions. You tell PHP what type of network transport you want to use by prefixing the transport to the name or IP address of the server you want to connect to.

```php
<?php

// Chapter 10: Stream and Network Programming
//
// Example 06: Using fsockopen()

// we will open a connection to the PHP Project's website, and download
// their front page
//
```

```
// note that what comes back is a redirect, and not the front-page itself
// this is an example of one of the many things that the http file wrapper
// automatically (and transparently) handles for us

$fp = fsockopen ("tcp://www.php.net", 80, $sock_errno, $sock_errmsg);
fwrite ($fp, "GET /\n");
while (!feof($fp))
{
    echo fgets($fp) . "\n";
}
fclose($fp);

?>
```

Sockets created using `fsockopen()` are automatically closed by PHP when your script ends. Sockets created using `pfsockopen()` are persistent.

Persistent Sockets

Sockets created using `pfsockopen()` remain open after your script has finished. When your next script calls `pfsockopen()` with the same hostname and port, PHP will reuse the socket that you opened last time—provided that the socket is still open.

PHP only persists sockets inside a single process.

- If you are using a CGI-BIN version of PHP, the next time your script runs, the old PHP process will have terminated. Your persistent socket will have been closed automatically by PHP when your script finished running.

- If you are using mod_php, or a FastCGI version of PHP (such as Zend's WinEnabler under IIS), there is a pool of reusable PHP engines. When your script runs, it might run inside the same copy of the engine as last time—or it might not. If your script runs inside a different copy of the engine, the call to `pfopensock()` will open up a new socket connection.

Remote servers (and especially by any firewalls in between) will automatically close persistent sockets if the socket isn't used for a period of time.

Timeouts When Opening a Socket

If you don't provide the timeout parameter to `fsockopen()`, PHP uses the value of `default_socket_timeout` from the `php.ini` settings.

The timeout parameter to `fsockopen()`, and the `default_socket_timeout` setting, only affect attempts to open the socket. This timeout is not used at all for read and write operations.

How Do I Use a Socket?

The PHP Streams architecture allows you to treat socket connections as you would another type of stream. To read from a socket, you can use `fread()` and others. To write to a socket, you can use `fwrite()` and others.

`fread()` and `fwrite()` are *binary safe*—you can use them to read and write any type of data that you need to.

Blocking Mode

By default, when PHP creates a new socket, it switches on blocking mode for that stream.

When blocking mode is on, any functions that attempt to read data from the stream will wait until there is some data available to be read—or until the socket is closed by the remote server.

```php
<?php

// Chapter 10: Stream and Network Programming
//
// Example 08: A blocked socket

// we will open a connection to the PHP Project's website, and attempt
// to read from the socket without having told the webserver what we
// want it to send us.
//
// this will block, and you should use CTRL+C to abort this script when
// you get bored enough

$fp = fsockopen("tcp://www.php.net", 80, $sock_errno, $sock_errmsg);

echo "Attempting to read from the stream ... this will not timeout\n";
echo "until the socket closes.  You should use CTRL+C to abort this\n";
echo "script when you're ready\n";

echo fgets($fp) . "\n";
fclose($fp);

?>
```

You can switch blocking mode off by using `stream_set_blocking()`:

```php
<?php

// Chapter 10: Stream and Network Programming
//
// Example 09: Switching off blocking mode
```

```php
// once again, we will make a connection to the PHP Project's webserver,
// and attempt to read from the socket without having told the webserver
// what page we want it to serve
//
// the difference this time is that we will switch off blocking mode first
//
// finally, we will dump the return value from fgets(), so you can see
// what fgets() returns when trying to read from a blocked stream

$fp = fsockopen("tcp://www.php.net", 80, $sock_errno, $sock_errmsg);
stream_set_blocking($fp, false);

echo "Attempting to read from the stream ... this will fail and return\n";
echo "immediately\n\n";

$result = fgets($fp);
fclose($fp);

echo "fgets() has returned:\n";

var_dump($result);

?>
```

Read/Write Timeouts

Instead of switching off blocking mode, you could use `stream_set_timeout()` to set a timeout on read/write operations instead.

```php
<?php

// Chapter 10: Stream and Network Programming
//
// Example 10: setting a timeout on a stream

// once again, we will make a connection to the PHP Project's webserver,
// and attempt to read from the socket without having told the webserver
// what page we want it to serve
//
// the difference this time is that we will set a read/write timeout of
// ten seconds on the stream
//
// finally, we will dump the return value from fgets(), so you can see
// what fgets() returns when stream operations timeout
```

```php
$fp = fsockopen("tcp://www.php.net", 80, $sock_errno, $sock_errmsg);
stream_set_timeout($fp, 10);

echo "Attempting to read from the stream ... this will timeout in 10 secs\n\n";

$result = fgets($fp);
fclose($fp);

echo "The fgets() has timed out, and returned:\n";

var_dump($result);

?>
```

Closing a Socket

When you have finished with a socket, you should close it as soon as possible.

The computer that your PHP script is running on can only open a limited number of sockets. The same is true for the network server at the other end of your socket. The sooner you can close your socket, the sooner the computer's operating system can recycle the network connection for someone else to use.

Use `fclose()` to close your socket:

```php
<?php

// Chapter 10: Stream and Network Programming
//
// Example 11: Using fclose()

// here, we create a stream using fsockopen(), and then demonstrate how
// to close it using fclose()
//
// once the stream has been closed, the file handle cannot be re-used
// without a new call to fopen() or fsockopen()

$fp = fsockopen ("tcp://www.php.net", 80, $sock_errno, $sock_errmsg);
fclose($fp);

echo "We have opened and closed the stream.  When we attempt to read from\n";
echo "the stream, PHP will output an error on your screen.\n";

echo fgets($fp);

?>
```

Further Reading

The seminal work on TCP/IP and socket programming is the series of books written by the late W. Richard Stevens.

- *UNIX Network Programming Volume 1: Networking APIs—Sockets and XTI*, W. Richard Stevens, Prentice Hall, ISBN 013490012X

- *UNIX Network Programming: The Sockets Networking API*, W. Richard Stevens, Bill Fenner, Andrew M. Rudoff, Prentice Hall, ISBN 0131411551

- *UNIX Network Programming: Interprocess Communications*, W. Richard Stevens, Prentice Hall, ISBN 0130810819

Individual network protocols are normally documented in the Request For Comments (RFC) series published by the Internet Engineering Task Force (IETF). For more details, see http://www.rfc-editor.org/.

Exam Prep Questions

1. The company you work for writes and sells a successful content management system (CMS). The CMS is written in PHP.

   Recently, your company has acquired the assets of one of your main competitors, including their CMS. The plan is to discontinue the rival CMS, and migrate all of its current customer base over to your CMS. However, this isn't going to happen until you've added some of the features that your CMS is currently lacking.

   The first feature that you have to add is a dead link checker. This handy little utility runs from the command-line, and checks a list of URLs to see whether they still work or not. Thanks to the new streams support in PHP 4.3, this should be very easy to do.

   Unfortunately, the first time you test your code, this error appears on the screen:

   ```
   Warning: fopen(): URL file-access is disabled in the server configuration in
   <file> on line 3
   Warning: fopen(URL): failed to open stream: no suitable wrapper could be
   found in <file> on line 3
   ```

   What is the cause of this error? Choose from one of the following.

   A. File wrappers don't allow you to access websites. You need to use the CURL extension for that.

   B. The web server is running behind a firewall, which is preventing access out to the Internet.

C. The web server's configuration file contains the setting 'allow_fopen_url=Off', which prevents the PHP file wrappers from working.

D. The php.ini configuration file contains the setting 'allow_fopen_url=Off', which prevents the PHP file wrappers from working.

The correct answer is **D**.

2. Now that you've fixed that little problem and are able to connect to remote websites from your PHP script, you're faced with another problem.

Your script's job is to determine whether or not a given URL is valid. How is your script going to do that?

Choose from one or more of the following options.

A. If the fopen() call fails, your script can assume that the remote website no longer exists.

B. Once you have opened the file wrapper, try reading from the file. If the read fails, then the remote web page no longer exists.

C. Check the metadata returned by opening the file, and use the HTTP status code returned by the server to determine whether or not the remote webpage still exists or not.

D. You can't use PHP to reliably check whether remote URLs exist or not. That's why all these tools are always written in Java.

The correct answers are **A** and **C**.

3. Decoding the status code contained in the file wrapper's metadata is an important task.

Where should you look to understand what the status code means?

Choose from one or more of the following:

A. The PHP Manual. It's well annotated, so even if the PHP developers forgot to list the status codes, you can be sure that a helpful PHP user has added them somewhere.

B. Microsoft.com. Internet Information Server is the web server of choice for many companies. Open standards are a nice ideal, but in the real world if code doesn't work for customers, you don't get paid.

C. W3C.org. They set the standards, and standards are important. By supporting the open standards, you can be sure that your code will work with most of the products out in the marketplace.

D Apache.org. The Apache web server is more popular than all the other web servers put together. If your code works with Apache, then it supports the market leader. And that's an important position to be in.

The correct answers are **B** and **C**.

4. Your boss was so impressed with your new dead link checker tool that he's given you responsibility for adding a larger feature to the CMS product proper.

He wants you to add file replication support.

For large websites, it can be very expensive to purchase a server powerful enough to cope with all the traffic and associated load. It's often much cheaper to purchase three or four smaller web servers, with a more powerful server acting as the admin server. New content is added to the admin server, and then pushed out to the smaller web servers.

Although most of the content lives in a shared database, original media files (PDF files, images, Word documents, and the like) are served directly off disk. This is partly a performance decision, and partly because some database servers have severe limits on their support for replicating large amounts of binary data.

You must write some code to copy files from the admin server to one or more web servers. There are no firewalls between the servers.

How would you do this? Choose one or more of the following options.

A. Put the media files into the database, and configure the web servers to retrieve the files from the database when they are needed.

B. Use file wrappers to write the media files out to a \\server\share network share.

C. Don't use file wrappers at all. Use NFS to mount the disks from the admin server on all the web servers, and access the files directly.

D. Use NFS to mount the disks from the web servers directly onto the admin server. Have the admin server write to each of the NFS mounts in turn.

The correct answers are **B** and **D**.

5. Customers are fickle things.

   Just as you have your new file replication code working, one of your major customers informs you that they have installed a firewall between the admin server and the web servers.

   This totally prevents your file replication code from working.

   Helpfully, the customer does allow outgoing HTTP connections through the firewall. You'll need to provide an alternative script, that uploads the files to the web servers through a HTTP connection. How are you going to do that?

   Choose from one or more of the following.

   A. File wrappers can't upload files via http. You'll have to use the CURL extension to achieve this.

   B. Just open a URL as a file and write to it. The whole point of file wrappers is to make operations like this easy.

   C. Use the stream context to tell the http file wrapper where to upload the file, and have a script on the web servers move the file from the uploads directory to their final destination.

   D. Use the FTP file wrapper to upload files directly to their final destination.

   The correct answer is **C**.

6. With file replication done and dusted, your boss is confident that he'll soon have customers migrating across from the discontinued CMS to your product. He'll have no trouble making his targets for the quarter, and earning his bonus.

   However, he needs one more feature porting across before he can be certain that customers will start migrating.

   Many sites like to keep in touch with their customers via a weekly newsletter. Many customers only come back to the website because there was something of interest to them in the newsletter. Being able to send newsletters—and being able to make those newsletters look professional—is an important feature.

   Your CMS doesn't support the concept of newsletters per se. But it does support the idea of packaging groups of files for downloading. If you could write a user-defined file wrapper that makes a MIME email look just like a ZIP file, it would then be very easy to add newsletter support.

   Sketch out a design for a file wrapper, which would allow a PHP script to add content, graphics, and other attachments to a MIME email.

11

Security

Terms You'll Need to Understand

- Data filtering
- register_globals
- SQL injection
- Command injection
- Cross-site scripting (XSS)
- Shared hosting
- safe_mode
- open_basedir

Techniques You'll Need to Master

- Validating client data
- Understanding the register_globals directive
- Escaping data used in SQL statements
- Escaping data used in shell commands
- Preventing cross-site scripting attacks
- Understanding the safe_mode directive
- Understanding the open_basedir directive

Data Filtering

Data filtering, the process of validating data and filtering out that which is invalid, is arguably the cornerstone of Web application security. The basic premise is quite simple: Never trust foreign data, especially data from the client.

There are two fundamentally different approaches to data filtering: the whitelist approach and the blacklist approach. With a whitelist approach, you assume data to be invalid unless it is proven otherwise (by meeting certain requirements of validity). With a blacklist approach, you assume data to be valid unless proven otherwise. Of course, the whitelist approach is stricter, and therefore more secure.

More pertinent than the principles of data filtering are the applications of it, many of which are covered in the following sections.

Register Globals

In PHP 4.2.0, the default value of the `register_globals` directive changed from `On` to `Off`. PHP professionals are now expected to write code that does not rely on `register_globals`.

When enabled, `register_globals` imports data from several different sources into the global namespace. Of particular interest to most developers is that the data from `$_POST`, `$_GET`, and `$_COOKIE` is available in regular global variables. For example, if a POST request contains a variable named `foo`, not only is `$_POST['foo']` created, but `$foo` is also created.

Although this behavior is simple and well documented, it carries serious implications with regard to data filtering. Whereas it is quite easy to determine that `$_POST['foo']` is something that needs to be validated prior to use, the origin of `$foo` is less clear when `register_globals` is enabled. In addition, if variables are not properly initialized, it is possible that you might use a variable sent from the client when you intend to be using a variable that you create yourself. A common example of this mistake is as follows:

```
if (authorized())
{
    $admin = true;
}

/* Later... */

if ($admin)
{
    /* Sensitive activity */
}
```

Because `$admin` is not properly initialized, a user can arbitrarily set its value by leveraging the behavior of `register_globals`. For example, the user can call the page with

`?admin=1` appended to the URL. This will cause `$admin` to be set to 1 at the beginning of the script. An important point is that a user has no control beyond the start of the script because a user can only manipulate the HTTP request. Once PHP begins execution, the request has been received, and a user can do nothing more to affect the pending response. This is why initializing your variables (and thereby overwriting any user-injected values) is such a good practice.

Of course, with proper programming practices, `register_globals` does not pose a significant risk. However, having `register_globals` enabled makes the magnitude of a mistake much greater, and it also makes it more difficult to identify foreign data.

The following guidelines are recommended, regardless of whether `register_globals` is enabled:

- Always initialize variables
- Develop with `error_reporting` set to `E_ALL`
- Filter all foreign data

SQL Injection

When querying a database, you will likely need to use foreign data in the construction of your SQL statement. For example, when storing data, you might be using values that the user supplies in an HTML form. When retrieving data, you might be using the user's username or some other client-supplied unique identifier as your primary key. Regardless of the reason, using foreign data in the construction of an SQL statement is something that poses a significant security risk. This cannot be avoided in most cases, but there are some best practices that can help mitigate the risk.

The first step, of course, is to properly filter the data, as just discussed. Most SQL injection vulnerabilities are a result of poor, or absent, data filtering. It is unlikely that valid data is going to pose a serious security risk.

With valid data, the only remaining concern is that you escape the data. This includes making sure that characters in the data aren't misinterpreted as being part of the SQL construct. If single quotes are properly escaped, this risk can be mitigated by always enclosing the data in single quotes within your SQL statement. For example,

```
$sql = "insert into foo values ('$bar')";
```

As long as `$bar` does not contain any unescaped single quotes, it cannot interfere with the construction of the SQL statement. Of course, there are other characters worth escaping, and depending on which database you use, PHP might have functions specifically designed for this task. For example, MySQL users can rely on `mysql_escape_string()` to do the escaping.

With some databases, certain data types (notably integers) cannot be enclosed in single quotes, but the data filtering for this type of data can be much stricter so that the other safeguards are less important.

Command Injection

Another dangerous activity is executing shell commands whereby the user has supplied a part of the command. Mitigating this risk is very similar to mitigating the risk of SQL injection, although there are some specific PHP functions that you should learn.

With properly filtered data, there are only two potential problems that you might encounter regarding shell commands:

1. There might be metacharacters that can be used to execute arbitrary commands.

2. If the data being used to construct a command is intended to be a single argument, there might be characters within the data that cause it to be interpreted as multiple arguments instead.

These problems are solved with `escapeshellcmd()` and `escapeshellarg()`, respectively. Data passed through `escapeshellcmd()` will be escaped such that it no longer poses a risk of arbitrary shell command execution. Data passed through `escapeshellarg()` can safely be used as a single argument.

Cross-Site Scripting

One of the most frequent vulnerabilities in modern PHP applications is cross-site scripting (XSS). As with most security concerns, proper data filtering can practically eliminate the risk of cross-site scripting. However, in this case, the real risk is when foreign data is used in your output and thereby potentially displayed to other users. This is fairly typical for applications such as Webmail, forums, wikis, and even 404 handlers.

The best defense of cross-site scripting is to use functions such as `htmlspecialchars()` or `htmlentities()` on data prior to displaying it. Of these two functions, `htmlentities()` is better for this purpose because it is more inclusive in terms of what entities it encodes.

This is a blacklist approach, but because there are a finite number of well-documented characters that have a special meaning within HTML, it is actually a pretty strong approach in this case. Of course, it is still best to be strict in your data filtering. If you are expecting a person's first name, should valid JavaScript make it through your data filtering? Hopefully you agree that this is not desirable.

Other functions such a `strip_tags()` (that attempts to remove all valid HTML and PHP) can also help in preventing cross-site scripting vulnerabilities, but this is an example of a somewhat weaker blacklist approach than what `htmlentities()` provides.

Shared Hosting

A common dilemma among PHP developers is achieving a satisfactory level of security on a shared host. There has been some effort to resolve some of the shared hosting security concerns, but none of these can help a shared host reach the level of security that you can achieve on a dedicated host.

Two particular attempts to address this problem are the safe_mode and open_basedir directives. The safe_mode directive effectively limits the files that a PHP script can open to those with the same ownership as the PHP script itself. This can help to prevent people from casually browsing the entire filesystem using a specially crafted PHP script, but it unfortunately cannot address situations in which other languages are used to achieve the same.

The open_basedir directive is similar—except that instead of relying on file permissions, it restricts the files that PHP can open to those within a certain directory. Thus, PHP cannot be used to open files outside of the directory specified by open_basedir. One somewhat tricky characteristic of open_basedir is that you can use partial names to match more than one directory. For example, a value of /tmp/foo will match both /tmp/foo and /tmp/foobar. If you want to restrict access to only /tmp/foo, you can use a trailing slash so that open_basedir is set to /tmp/foo/.

Both of these directives require administrative access, of course; otherwise, a developer could simply override these settings.

Exam Prep Questions

1. Which of the following data filtering methods can be described as a whitelist approach?

    A. Make sure that a username does not contain backticks or angled brackets.

    B. Only allow alphanumerics and underscores in a username.

    C. Pass all incoming data through strip_tags().

    D. Use htmlentities() to escape potentially malicious characters.

    Answer **B** is correct. Answer A is incorrect because this assumes that any username without backticks or angled brackets is valid. Answer C is incorrect because this only removes HTML and PHP tags, assuming everything else to be valid. Answer D is incorrect because htmlentities() only encodes HTML entities and is not intended to filter data at all.

2. With register_globals enabled, which of the following practices is particularly important?

    A. Initialize all variables.

    B. Filter all foreign data.

    C. Escape all data used in SQL statements.

    D. Escape all data prior to output.

    Answer **A** is correct. Answers B, C, and D are incorrect because these practices are not dependent on whether register_globals is enabled.

3. What are the two most important practices to mitigate the risk of an SQL injection vulnerability?

    A. Disabling `register_globals` and enabling `safe_mode`.

    B. Enabling `safe_mode` and filtering any data used in the construction of the SQL statement.

    C. Filtering and escaping any data used in the construction of the SQL statement.

    D. Disabling `register_globals` and escaping any data used in the construction of the SQL statement.

    Answer **C** is correct. With properly filtered data, escaping any metacharacters that remain can mitigate the remaining risks. Answers A, B, and D are incorrect because `register_globals` does not directly affect the risk of SQL injection, and `safe_mode` is unrelated.

4. If `$foo` is anticipated to be a string, what modification made to the following query will mitigate the risk of an SQL injection vulnerability?

    ```
    $sql = "insert into mytable values ($foo)";
    ```

    A. Specify the column name in the SQL statement.

    B. Remove the parentheses surrounding `$foo`.

    C. Replace the parentheses surrounding `$foo` with single quotes.

    D. Add single quotes around `$foo`.

    Answer **D** is correct. Answer A is incorrect because specifying the column name does not affect the behavior of the SQL statement. Answers B and C are incorrect because the parentheses are required.

5. What is the purpose of the `escapeshellcmd()` function?

    A. To prepare data so that it can be used as a single argument in a shell command.

    B. To remove malicious characters.

    C. To escape metacharacters, so that they can't be used to execute arbitrary commands.

    D. To prevent cross-site scripting attacks.

    Answer **C** is correct. Answer A is incorrect because `escapeshellcmd()` does not attempt to solve this problem. Answer B is incorrect because `escapeshellcmd()` does not actually remove characters. Answer D is incorrect because escaping data to protect against cross-site scripting is much different than escaping data to be used in a shell command.

6. What is the purpose of the `escapeshellarg()` function?

   A. To prepare data so that it can be used as a single argument in a shell command.

   B. To remove malicious characters.

   C. To escape metacharacters, so that they can't be used to execute arbitrary commands.

   D To remove arguments from a shell command.

   Answer **A** is correct. Answers B and D are incorrect because `escapeshellarg()` does not remove characters. Answer C is incorrect because `escapeshellarg()` does not attempt to solve this problem.

7. When is cross-site scripting a heightened risk?

   A. When storing data submitted by the user.

   B. When displaying foreign data.

   C. When executing a shell command.

   D. When opening a remote URL.

   Answer **B** is correct. When displaying foreign data that is not properly escaped, you can inadvertently expose your users to significant risk. Answer A is incorrect because storing data poses no immediate threat, even though this might result in a cross-site scripting vulnerability later. Answers C and D are incorrect because these activities are unrelated.

8. Which of the following functions can be used to escape data such that it can be displayed without altering the appearance of the original data?

   A. `htmlspecialchars()`

   B. `addslashes()`

   C. `escapeshellargs()`

   D. `urlencode()`

   Answer **A** is correct because `htmlspecialchars()` will convert special characters to HTML entities that will display correctly in any Web client. Answer B is incorrect because `addslashes()` only escapes single quotes. Answer C is incorrect because `escapeshellargs()` is only helpful when dealing with shell command arguments. Answer D is incorrect because URL encoding is not interpreted by Web clients except in the context of URLs.

9. What is the purpose of the `open_basedir` directive?

   A. To indicate the directory that `include()` calls will use as a base.

   B. To restrict file open access to a specific directory.

   C. To set the working directory.

   D. To allow additional file open access than that granted by `safe_mode`.

   Answer **B** is correct. Answer A is incorrect because the behavior of `include()` is unchanged. Answer C is incorrect because the working directory does not depend on `open_basedir`. Answer D is incorrect because `open_basedir` is not affected by whether `safe_mode` is enabled.

10. Which of the following activities can `safe_mode` help prevent?

    A. Browsing the filesystem with a specially crafted PHP script.

    B. Writing a Bash shell script to read session data.

    C. Browsing the filesystem with a specially crafted Perl script.

    D. Accessing another user's database.

    Answer **A** is correct because you'll only be able to browse files that have the same ownership as your PHP script. Answers B and C are incorrect because `safe_mode` cannot affect scripts written in other languages. Answer D is incorrect because `safe_mode` does not attempt to prevent database access.

12

Debugging and Performance

MAKING MISTAKES IS HUMAN, and so is fixing them. In your day-to-day programming adventures, it's inevitable to introduce bugs in your PHP code, especially when you're writing very complex applications with tens of thousands of lines of code spread across tens of files.

When you're prototyping an application, being able to avoid common programming mistakes is important to ensure that your code will be well-written from the very start. In this chapter, we'll provide you with some guidelines on writing efficient code, debugging faulty scripts, and identifying bottlenecks when performance becomes an issue for both you and your clients.

Terms You'll Need to Understand

- Bug
- Coding standard
- Code readability
- Comparison operators
- Performance
- Caching
- Portability

Techniques You'll Need to Master

- Writing readable code
- Proper commenting
- Comparing heterogeneous data
- Debugging

- Identifying and preventing performance bottlenecks
- Preventing performance issues
- Improving database performance
- Using content and bytecode caching

Coding Standards

Writing your code in a structured manner is, perhaps, the smartest decision you can make. Although there aren't any predefined coding standards that everyone in the programming community recognizes as better than the rest, deciding from the very beginning on a set of conventions will go a long way toward helping you make fewer mistakes.

Documenting your code is particularly important. To make this job—probably at the top of the Ten Most Hated Tasks of programmers worldwide—a bit easier, you can even use one of the many automated tools available on the market, such as PHPDocumentor, which can extract documentation directly from your code if you structure your comments in a particular way.

Regardless of how you introduce them in your applications, good comments and documentation will make sharing your code with other members of your team easier, as well as make sure that you'll remember what it does when you get back from that three-week vacation. Remember, preventing bugs is *much* better than hunting for them.

Extra whitespace and empty lines, although unimportant as far as the functionality of your code is concerned, can be an extremely valuable tool for writing better code:

```
if ($foo == 'bar')
{
    $i = 0;

    /**
   * foreach loop, get the content out of it
     */

    foreach ( …. )
    {
    }
}
```

By separating your code into logical groups, your source will be cleaner and easier to read. Also, indenting each line according to the code block it belongs to helps you figure out immediately what the structure of your script is.

Flattening `if` Statements

Consider the following snippet of code:

```
if ($is_allocated)
{
    if ($has_been_mangled)
    {
        if ($foo == 5)
        {
            print "foo is 5";
        }
        else
        {
            print "You entered the wrong data!";
        }
    }
    else
    {
        return false;
    }
}
else
{
    return false;
}
```

As you can see, the many nested `if` statements here cause the code to look very busy and difficult to read. An easy way to improve the situation consists of "flattening" your `if` statements so that you can achieve the minimum level of indentation without compromising either the functionality of your code or its performance. The preceding script, for example, could be rewritten as follows:

```
if (!$is_allocated)
{
    return false;
}

if (!$has_been_mangled)
{
    return false;
}

if ($foo == 5)
{
    print "foo is 5";
```

```
}
else
{
    print "You entered the wrong data!";
}
```

This approach gives you a better structure with fewer levels of nesting so that your code is easier to understand. Note that the type of operations performed is pretty much the same as before—and the elimination of two `else` statements will make the code easier to parse for the interpreter.

Splitting Single Commands Across Multiple Lines

One of the great things about PHP is that it doesn't require you to write a single statement all on one line of code. In fact, any statement can be split across an arbitrary number of lines without any change in its functionality—provided, of course, that the split doesn't take place in the middle of a text string. This is particularly useful when you have a complex line of code that spans a large number of characters:

```
$db->query("select foo,
            bar,
            mybar as foobar
            from tbl1
            where tbl1.mybar='foo'");
```

This database query is split over several lines. The main advantage here is that you can immediately see what the query does, which tables are involved, and which conditions you are placing in the `where` clause. If the same query had been placed all on the same line, understanding its purpose would have taken a lot more effort, and the risk of introducing new bugs by modifying it would have been greater.

Concatenation Versus Substitution

If you are inserting data into a long string—such as a database query—you can use the concatenation operator, but doing so often limits your ability to read the query properly:

```
$db->query
("insert into foo(id,bar)
values('".addslashes($id).
"','".addslashes($bar)."')");
```

On the other hand, you could just use one of the `printf()` functions to do the job for you:

```
$db->query(sprintf("insert into foo(id,bar) values('%s','%s')",
  addslashes($id),
  addslashes($bar)
));
```

As you can see, the entire statement is now a lot easier to read, although you will lose some performance by switching to `sprintf()` from the concatenation operator, which is native to the PHP interpreter and doesn't require the execution of any external libraries. The literals in the string passed to `sprintf()` will be substituted with the values of the parameters passed afterwards in the order in which they appear in the call. Combined with the ability to split your commands over several lines, this approach can enhance readability to a large degree.

Choose Your Opening Tags Carefully

Mixing PHP and HTML code is one of the characteristics of PHP that make it both easy to use and powerful, although it's easy to abuse this capability and come up with code that is difficult to read.

When writing code for an application that could run on heterogeneous systems, it's always a good idea to be very careful about which opening tag styles you use. In Chapter 1, "The Basics of PHP," we mentioned that there are several of them, but only the canonical tags `<?php ?>` are fully portable. Short tags (which include the echo tag `<?=`) and ASP tags can all be turned off through PHP configuration directives.

Thus, the following

```
<?php print "Testing 1 2 3" ?>
```

is longer than

```
<?= "Testing 1 2 3" ?>
```

But not quite as portable. Note, also, that there is a subtle difference between `print` and `echo`. Although they are both language constructs, the former acts as a function—meaning that it actually returns a value (always a Boolean `True`)—whereas the latter does not. Thus, the following code is valid, although quite pointless:

```
<?php echo print (10) ?>
```

One Equal, Two Equals, Three Equals

How often did you write the following code?

```
if ($a = 5)
{
    print "a is 5";
}
```

If you're like most programmers, the answer is an unfortunate "often." The problem here is caused by the fact that the `if` statement allows for *any* operations to take place inside its condition—including assignments. Thus, the preceding line is not technically incorrect, but it's obviously not what the author intended to perform, as it will always be evaluated to true, making the `if` statement pointless and, what's worse, changing the value of `$a`.

Clearly, the statement should have been written as follows:

```
if ($a == 5
{
    print "a is 5";
}
```

In this case, the condition is a comparison operator, and it will be evaluated as true only if the value of $a is 5.

There is, luckily, a very easy way to avoid this mistake once and for all, without any possibility of ever slipping again: make sure that the condition is written in such a way that it cannot possibly be misinterpreted:

```
if (5 == $a)
{
        print "a is 5";
}
```

With this approach, if you mistakenly only use one equal sign instead of two, as in 5 = $a, the interpreter will print out an error because you can't assign anything to an immediate value. If you make a habit of writing all your conditions this way, you will never fall in the assignment trap again!

There's Equal and *Equal*

As we mentioned in Chapter 1, PHP is a loosely typed language. This means that, under the right circumstances, it will automatically juggle data types to perform its operations according to how programmers are most likely to want it to.

There are scenarios, however, in which this is not a desirable approach, and you want, instead, PHP to be strict and literal in the way it compares data. Consider, for example, what would happen if you were dealing with information coming from a patient's medical record. In this situation, you'll want to make sure that nothing is left to chance and that PHP doesn't attempt to interpret user input in too liberal a way.

Generally speaking, it's always a good idea to use the identity operators (=== and !==) whenever you know that a value has to be of a certain type:

```
if ($a !== 0) {
    echo '$a is not an integer zero';
}
```

Testing for Resource Allocation

One of the most common mistakes that causes code to become unreliable consists of using external resources without ensuring that they are available. For example, look at the following code:

```
$res = mysql_query("select foo from bar");
while ($row = mysql_fetch_array($res))
{
    print $row['foo']."<br>";
}
```

See what's wrong? The author doesn't test for the query's failure before moving on to perform other tasks that use the resource returned by `mysql_query()`. The query could fail for a number of reasons, even though it is syntactically correct—for example, the server might be unavailable, or there could be a network interruption. What's worse in this particular case, the MySQL extension does not cause a fatal error if a query cannot be executed. Therefore, the script moves on, and a cascade of additional problems could be caused by this initial blunder.

If, on the other end, error conditions are properly tested for, this issue doesn't even present itself:

```
if (!$res = mysql_query("select foo from bar"))
{
    /**
    * no valid result, log/print error, mysql_error() will tell you
    */
}
else
{
    while ($row = mysql_fetch_array($res))
    {
        print $row['foo']."<br>";
    }
}
```

It's undoubtedly hard to write an `if` statement every time you execute a query—but also necessary if you are serious about error management. To make things a bit easier on yourself (and your entire team), you could adopt one of the many abstraction layers available or write one yourself. This way, the actual error management can be performed in a centralized location (the abstraction layer), and you won't have to write too much code.

It's important to keep in mind that this process is required whenever you interact with an external resource, be it a database, a file, or a network connection.

Starting with PHP 5, you can use other error-control structures known as *exceptions*. However, remember that these are not available in PHP 4 and, therefore, cannot be used to solve a problem that appears in the exam.

Ternary Operators and `if` Statements

`if` statements are necessary control structures for all but the simplest of PHP scripts. As a result, sometimes they will tend to be very complex, even if you nest them on various levels.

Luckily, the ternary conditional operator that you saw in Chapter 1 can be used to simplify the use of `if` statements by embedding them directly in a larger expression. For example, consider the following snippet of code:

```
function is_my_country($country)
{
    if (strlen($country) == 3)
    {
        return 1;
    }
    else
    {
        return 0;
    }
}
```

It could also be written as

```
function is_my_country($country) {
    return (strlen($country)==3) ? 1 : 0;
}
```

As you can see, the function is much shorter than the `if` statement in the preceding example. This can be very valuable if you're dealing with a complex piece of code such as the following:

```
$db->query(sprintf("insert into foo(f1,f2,f3) values('%s','%s','%s')",
    (isset($_SESSION['foobar'])) ? 'yes' : 'no',
    (isset($_POST['myfoo']) && $_POST['myfoo']!='') ? $_POST['myfoo'] : 'no',
    'foo'));
```

A call such as the preceding one would have been a lot more complex if it had been written using traditional `if` statements—not to mention that you would have needed either a number of new variables to hold the information, or a different set of function calls for each possible scenario.

Logging and Debugging

Displaying error messages to the browser is a problem from many points of view. First, you're letting your visitors know that something in your code is broken, thus shaking their confidence in the solidity of your website. Second, you're exposing yourself to potential security vulnerabilities because some of the information outputted might be used to hack into your system. Third, you're preventing yourself from finding out what error occurred so that you can fix it.

A good solution to this problem consists of changing your `php.ini` setting so that the errors are not displayed to the screen, but stored in a log file. This is done by turning `display_errors` to `off` and `log_errors` to `on`, as well as setting a log file where the error messages are stored through the `error_log` option. You can open a shell and use `tail -f` to follow the PHP log.

If you want to go a step further, you could use the `set_error_handler()` function to define your own error handlers and log additional information that you might find useful when trying to troubleshoot the problem.

Naturally, you can also use the error-suppression operator `@` to prevent PHP from displaying or logging the error. Although this is an easy way to solve the problem, it could lead to problems when using in production scenarios in which you *do* need to find out when an error occurs so that you can fix it.

Using Debuggers

Ultimately, not all bugs can be solved just by staring really hard at the code (although it often helps to). In some cases, you just need to "see" the program running to discover what's causing it not to perform properly. What you need is a debugger.

A lot of debuggers exist, starting with the ancient DBG (now integrated into NuSphere's PHPEd) and progressing to APD, XDebug and the debugger that's integrated into the Zend Studio IDE. Most debuggers have the capability to set breakpoints on specific lines in your code and watch points where you can watch the global scope of your PHP variables.

Using a debugger, you can step through each line of your application and see exactly how it flows. As such, you should definitely be familiar with one because some day you're *definitely* going to need one.

Optimizing Performance

Performance is a "happy problem" until the day it falls in your lap. Nothing can ruin your day like a pointy-haired manager screaming in your ears because the website is not responding well to an increase in traffic.

Although it won't have an immediate impact on your ability to go live, measuring the performance of a website is an important step that will come in handy on the day in which you will need to troubleshoot it.

Hardware Issues

Naturally, the easiest way to help a system that is ailing because of too much traffic is to throw more hardware at it. You could increase your onboard RAM or the speed of your hard disks, or you could even add another server altogether.

Another good idea is to ensure that your data is all stored in the right place. By saving the logs on a separate disk or partition than where your main application files are stored, you can help the operating system optimize its caching mechanisms and provide higher performance.

Although a well-configured computer is a great starting point as far as ensuring that your application is performing to the best of its capabilities, eventually you are going to find that an alternative solution is required since you obviously can't simply add new servers to your farm indefinitely.

Web Server Issues

Proper web server configuration goes a long way toward improving performance. A good starting point is to turn off reverse DNS resolution since you don't need it at the time when your web server is simply logging information about site access. You can always perform that operation offline when you analyze your logs.

It's also a good idea to familiarize yourself with how the web server you're using works. For example, Apache 1.3.x is a forking web server—meaning that it creates copies of its own process as children. Each child process waits for a connection (for example from a web browser) and, if there are more connections than available idle children, the server creates new ones as needed.

In its default configuration, Apache pre-forks 5 children and has a maximum of 150. If you consider that each child requires between 2 and 5 megabytes of memory to run (assuming your scripts don't require even more), this could easily lead to a performance bottleneck if the traffic on your server goes up. At maximum load, 150 child processes could require between 300MB and 750MB of RAM. And, if you run out of physical memory, the operating system will switch to its virtual memory, which is significantly slower.

This problem can also become self-compounding. As more and more child processes are created and the system is forced to rely increasingly on virtual memory, the average response time will increase. This, in turn, will cause even more child processes to be created to handle new connections, eventually exhausting all your system resources and causing connection failures.

As a result, a careful read of your web server's documentation is probably one of the cheapest (and smartest) investments that you can make. Do take the time to tune the appropriate configuration options for minimum and maximum clients and only compile or activate those web server modules you really need in order to save memory consumption.

Avoid Overkill

If you're dealing with a mixture of static and dynamic content, it's a good idea to keep things simple and let a lightweight web server handle the static data. Because you don't need any of the advanced features provided by PHP and Apache, using a different server that requires fewer system resources to run will increase your performance. You can even move the static data to a different server altogether and neatly divide the work across multiple machines.

Zip It Up

HTML is a very verbose language. As a result, web pages are often rather large—although maybe not as large as, say, a video or audio stream. Still, even a 20KB page will take its sweet time across a slow dial-up connection.

PHP makes it possible to compress the output of a script so that it can travel faster to the user. This can be done in a number of ways—for example, you can enable the GZIP buffer handler in your `php.ini` file or turn it on directly from within your scripts:

```
ob_start("ob_gzhandler");
```

Naturally, the output of your scripts will only be compressed if the browser that is requesting the document supports the GZIP compression standard.

Database Optimizations

Although we've briefly discussed databases in Chapter 9, "PHP and Databases," it's a good idea to start thinking about them in terms of performance. When you execute a database query, you depend on an external resource to perform an operation and, if that operation is slow, your entire website will suffer.

There is no predetermined "maximum number of queries" that you should use when writing database-driven websites. Generally speaking, the higher the number, the slower a page will be, but a single badly written query can slow down a web page more than 20 well-written ones. As a general guideline, most developers try to keep the number of queries performed in every page below five—however, many websites use a higher number without suffering any significant performance degradation.

Optimizing the tables that your queries use is the first step toward ensuring fast data access. This means that you will have to normalize your database so that a particular field is stored only in one table and each table is properly linked with the others through foreign keys. In addition, you will have to ensure that all your tables have been properly indexed to ensure that the queries you execute can take full advantage of the DBMS's capability to organize data in an efficient way.

Naturally, your optimizations should not come at the expense of security. Always make sure that you escape all user input properly (as discussed in Chapter 9) and that the statements you perform are safe even if the database itself changes.

For example, consider this simple query:

```
INSERT into my_table
values (10, 'Test')
```

This query expects that `my_table` will always have two fields. If you extend it to include additional columns, the query will fail. This might seem like a far-fetched scenario, but it really isn't. A complex application often includes hundreds, or even thousands, of queries, and it's easy to forget that one exists when making such sweeping changes.

On the other hand, it's easy enough to fix this problem by simply rewriting the query so that it specifies *which* fields it intends to insert data in:

```
INSERT into my_table (id, name)
values (10, 'Test')
```

In this case, it will be a lot more difficult for an error to crop up—but by no means impossible. If the new fields you have added to my_table do not accept null values and have no default values defined, the query will still fail because the database won't accept empty columns. Thus, you really have to be careful when making changes to your database!

Keep Your Code Simple

If you're coming from a Java background, you might be used to writing a large infrastructure of classes that rely on each other to perform a particular task.

Don't try this with PHP! PHP's OOP features work best when your framework is small and efficient. Creating objects in PHP is a rather slow process, and, as such, it should be used conscientiously.

Caching Techniques

Sometimes, it's just not possible to optimize your code beyond a certain point. It might be that your queries are too complicated or that you depend on a slow external resource, such as a web service, over which you have no control.

In these cases, you might want to think about using a *caching solution* that "saves" the output of an operation and then allows you to access it without performing that operation again.

There are several types of cache; for example, you can save the results of a database query, or even an entire web page. The latter means that you generate your pages normally at predetermined intervals and save them in the cache. When a page is requested by a user, it is actually retrieved from the cache instead of being generated from scratch.

You can find several packages in the PEAR repository that are useful for output caching of various type. Naturally, there are also commercial solutions that perform a similar task, such as the ones provided by Zend.

Bytecode Caches

When PHP runs your scripts, it does so in two steps. First, it *parses* the script itself, transforming it into a sort of intermediate language referred to as *bytecode*. Then, it actually interprets the bytecode (which is simpler than PHP itself) and executes it. If your scripts don't change between one execution and the next, the first step could easily be skipped, and only the second step would have to be taken.

This is what "bytecode caches" do. They are usually installed as simple extensions to PHP that act in a completely transparent way, caching the bytecode versions of your script and skipping the parsing step unless it is necessary—either because the script has never been parsed before (and, therefore, can't be in the cache yet) or because the original script has changed and the cache needs refreshing.

A number of commercial and open-source bytecode caches (also called *accelerators*) are available on the market, such as the one contained in the Zend Performance Suite, or the open-source APC. Most often, they also modify the bytecode so as to optimize it by removing unnecessary instructions.

Bytecode caching should always be the last step in your optimization process because no matter how efficient your code is, it's always going to provide you with the same performance boost. And, as a result, it could trick you into a false sense of security that would prevent you from looking at the other performance optimization techniques available.

Exam Prep Questions

1. How can the following line of code be improved?

   ```
   $db->query("insert into foo values($id,$bar)");
   ```

   A. Use `addslashes` and `sprintf` to avoid security holes and make the code cleaner

   B. Split the query over several lines

   C. Use `mysql_query()` instead of `$db->query()`

   D. Define the table fields that will be affected by the INSERT statement

   E. Use `mysql_query()` instead of `$db->query()` and `addslashes` to avoid security holes

   Answers **A**, **B**, and **D** are correct. First of all, you need to ensure that the query is secure; this is done by executing `addslashes` (or the equivalent function for your DBMS of choice) to prevent scripting attacks. If your query is long, it's not a bad idea to split it over several lines to get a better overview of your code. Use `sprintf()` where possible to make the code cleaner. Finally it's always a good idea to define the table fields that will be filled by an INSERT statement to prevent unexpected errors if the table changes.

2. You developed a big application accessed by several thousand users at the same time. Suddenly, your web server stops responding and users are getting connection errors. What could have happened?

    A. The database server was terminated because of the unusually high amount of database accesses.

    B. The web server was misconfigured so that it ran into virtual memory usage and consequent resource starvation because of too many child processes.

    C. You didn't optimize your code design properly.

Answer **B** is correct. Although it could be possible that the database server was killed because of the many requests from the users, they should at least be able to see the HTML pages from the website because the web server would still be running. If connections are timing out, it is likely that the server ran into swap space because of misconfiguration of the number of concurrent web server child processes and crashed because of resource starvation.

3. You are in a team of developers working on a number of different business applications. Your project manager tells you that in two weeks another three PHP developers will join the team and that you have to ensure that they will be ready to dive in to the current PHP code without problems. What could you do?

    A. Write proper end user documentation on how to use the web front end.

    B. Write proper end user documentation and generate proper PHPDoc comments inside the code to get an API documentation.

    C. The absence of documentation will actually encourage the new developers to delve more deeply into the code.

Answer **B** is correct—or, at least, as correct as you can get in a general situation. The key here is that you should write proper documentation at the same time as you're writing your code. You could then use a tool such as PHPDocumentor to generate a nicely formatted API documentation in HTML or PDF and make it available to any new developers who join your team.

4. Suppose that you are receiving input from the user in the form of the string "0mydeviceid" for a field for which you only allow valid numeric values. You want to test if this variable is equal to 0 and, if it isn't, output an error. Which comparison operation should you use?

    A. (0 = "0mydeviceid")

    B. (0 == "0mydeviceid")

    C. (0 === "0mydeviceid")

    D. None of the above

Answer **D** is correct. Because PHP is automatically trying to convert the string "0mydeviceid" to 0 when comparing it with the equal operator == , your condition in answer B evaluates to true even though the user input is *not* a valid numeric value. The expression in answer C, on the other hand, correctly determines that the user input is not a valid integer—but that will always be the case because you're likely to always receive user input in the form of a string—so, even if that string can be converted to an integer value, the identity test will fail.

13

Getting Ready for the Certification Exam

IN THE PREVIOUS CHAPTERS, YOU LEARNED about the PHP language and the specific topics that are covered in the Zend PHP Certification. In this chapter, you will learn other aspects of the exam such as how the exam is constructed and the various stages involved in the certification process—thus limiting any surprises you might encounter when taking the exam and assisting you in using your time efficiently, maximizing your efforts toward attaining your educational goal.

What the Exam Tests

The Zend PHP Certification formally confirms the recognition of specific abilities and skills acquired and developed by the examinee. In other words, how predictably is the person likely to perform when applying PHP technology to a business problem? Have the examinees reached a predefined minimum standard in both academic and practical experience needed to produce quality work?

How to Register

The Zend PHP Certification tests are delivered using a state-of–the-art electronic testing service provided by Pearson VUE. With over 3,500 test centers worldwide, finding a test center near you is simple and fast. Using the Test Center Locator available on the top menu of Pearson VUE's website (http://www.vue.com/) choose IT Certification as the Testing Category and select Zend from the Testing Program menu. You will be presented with a list of countries where you begin to narrow down your search, finally finding a test center nearest your location.

There are three different methods you can use to register for the certification exam. Regardless of the method you choose, a Zend.com username is mandatory for registration and is used for syncing your exam results with your Zend database profile. A Zend.com username can be obtained online at http://zend.com/add_user.php simply by filling in a few details. Using an incorrect username when registering at Pearson VUE might result in delays processing exam results and certification delivery.

Registration via Pearson VUE Call Center

If you would like to talk to a Pearson VUE representative in order to register and schedule your test, call centers are available in the United States and Canada from 7:00 a.m. to 7:00 p.m. (Central Time), Monday through Friday. Non-U.S. call centers are available in the Asia-Pacific, Europe, Middle East, and Africa regions. These call centers operate from 9:00 a.m. to 6:00 p.m., local time, Monday through Friday. For a complete list of call centers and phone numbers, visit http://www.vue.com/contact/zend/.

A Pearson VUE representative will inform you of Test Center locations and availability and schedule a time for the certification test at your convenience.

Registration via the Person VUE Website

Probably by far the most popular and convenient way to register and schedule a certification test is by using the Pearson VUE website, which can be located at http://www.vue.com/. You must first create an account prior to scheduling your test location and time. By clicking on the Create Account button positioned on the top left side of the home page, you will be asked to choose a Testing Category and Testing Program, where IT Certification and Zend should be selected, respectively. On the next few pages, you will be required to enter personal information, including your name and contact information. When asked for your Zend.com username, make sure that what you provide is accurate because this information is used at Zend when processing your exam data. Any imprecision will lead to manual processing of your information and therefore delay the arrival of your certificate.

After a Pearson VUE web account is created, scheduling your certification test time and location is conveniently accomplished by using the online interface that directs you through the various stages.

Registration at the Test Center

Some Test Centers allow a walk-in registration process. The Test Center will gather all necessary information and enter the candidate into the system to schedule an exam. Not all Test Centers provide this service, and you should call first to verify. Test Center telephone numbers and locations can be found on the Pearson VUE website at http://www.vue.com.

What to Expect at the Test Center

You should arrive at the Test Center on your scheduled day 15 minutes before your test begins. This will provide you and the Test Center sufficient time in which to sign you in and prepare any material necessary for the event. Upon your arrival, the Test Center coordinator who welcomes you will request two forms of identification. At least one piece of identification should include a recent photo.

You will be requested to surrender personal belongings that include, but are not limited to books, cell phones, and bags. They will be stored in a secure place for the duration of the test.

The Zend PHP Certification is a closed-book exam. No software is permitted for use in the exam, and there will not be any Internet access. You will however be provided with some paper and a pen for taking notes and performing calculations that might help during the time of the test. At the end of the test, the paper and pen are returned to the Test Center coordinator. In some Test Centers, an erasable plastic board and a marker are provided instead of the paper and pen.

How the Exam Works

The Zend PHP Certification is a 90-minute exam with a total of 70 questions. Before starting the exam, you will be provided with Exam Instructions, a Nondisclosure Agreement, and a short five-question survey. Familiarizing yourself with these pre-exam procedures and items can save you precious time, which is better used answering test questions.

Exam Instructions

The instructions provided to the examinee prior to the exam (valid during the time of this publication) are

- The questions are relevant to PHP versions 4 and above (up to version 4.3.6.).
- Unless stated otherwise, the recommended php.ini file must be assumed.
- When asked to supply a function name, do **not** include the parenthesis.
- Your answers should reflect PHP's case-sensitivity rules.

NDA (NONDISCLOSURE AGREEMENT)

The following nondisclosure agreement is supplied before the exam questions. It is encouraged that you read the NDA ahead of time rather than during the test. This will not only save time, but will also give you one less item to worry about before you begin your one-and-a-half-hour long test.

NONDISCLOSURE AGREEMENT AND GENERAL TERMS OF USE FOR ZEND PHP CERTIFICATION EXAMS, AND LOGO USAGE AGREEMENT

This exam is Zend Technologies Ltd.'s ("Zend") proprietary and confidential information and is protected by trade secret laws and other applicable laws. It is made available to you, the examinee, solely for the purpose of becoming certified in the technical area referenced in the title of this exam. You are expressly prohibited from copying, disclosing, publishing, reproducing, or transmitting this exam, in whole or in part (including any question or answer thereto), in any form or by any means, verbal or written, electronic or mechanical, for any purpose, without the prior express written permission of Zend.

Zend may, at its sole discretion, designate a logo for limited use by those individuals who have passed this exam (the "Logo"). The Logo is personal and may only be used by you and no other person or entity. You may use the Logo only on your personal business cards, letterhead, personal website, and your resume and not in any other form. You are prohibited from displaying or using the Logo in any way that may imply that you are an employee or otherwise related to, or endorsed by, Zend. The Logo only relates to that level of certification that you have achieved. You may not modify or otherwise alter or change the Logo. In the event your certification expires or is otherwise terminated, you will immediately cease use of the Logo.

Viewing Backward and Forward

During the exam, the examinee may page back and forward at any time. Even after the completion of the entire exam, you may go back to review, change, and edit answers. Once the End Exam button has been pressed, the exam is processed and no changes can be made.

Reviewing Your Answers

If you are unsure about a certain question during the test or would like to remind your-self to come back to a question at the end of the test, you may use the Review feature. This is a recommended and time-saving feature. It appears as a review check box on the upper left-hand corner of the exam delivery application. Checking this box will mark the question for review, and at the end of the exam, a summary of all the questions marked by you will be displayed with the option to go back and iterate through only those questions.

Your Comments

Examinees are able to leave comments throughout the duration of the exam by either clicking the comment button at the bottom of the screen or pressing ALT+M, which opens a comment window. It is suggested that you only leave comments after you have completed all the questions. No extra time will be added to the exam for the time taken to write comments.

What Kinds of Questions Are Asked?

The certification test consists of four different question types: single choice, multiple choice, fill in the blanks, and open questions.

Single Choice Questions

A single choice question begins with a question or comment and is sometimes accom-panied with some PHP code or code output. The examinee is requested to choose a single answer from a given selection of between two and six answers. There is only one correct answer for these types of questions and only one answer can be marked. You will normally notice answers that might seem correct but because of some small detail, they are not. Pay attention to exactly what is being asked!

An example of a single choice question is

What does PHP stand for?

A. People Helping People

B. PHP Hypertext Preprocessor

C. PHP Hypertext Preprocessing

D. Perl Hypertext Preprocessor

Figure 13.1 shows an example of how a single choice question would appear in an exam.

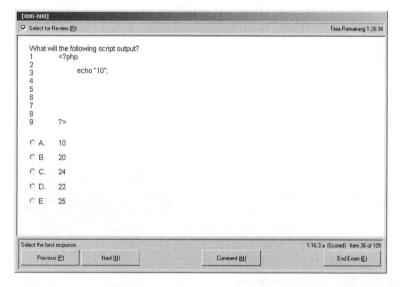

Figure 13.1   A single choice question.

Multiple Choice Questions

Constructed similar to single choice questions though with one major difference; the multiple choice questions have between two and four correct answers. The examinee is notified of the number of correct answers that should be checked. This tip might not exist in future versions on the PHP certification—in which case, it will be up to the examinee to decide how many answers he thinks are correct and should be marked.

An example of a multiple choice question is

Which of the following are directives in the `php.ini` file? (Choose three.)

A. `session.save_handler`

B. `asp_tags`

C. `output_buffering`

D. `flush`

Figure 13.2 shows an example of how a multiple choice question would appear in an exam.

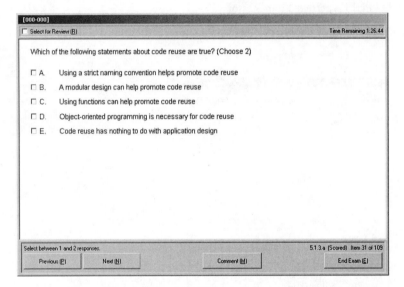

Figure 13.2   A multiple choice question.

Fill in the Blanks Questions

The examinee is provided with one or more sentences that have had parts extracted and replaced with underscores. The examinee then chooses the most appropriate set of extractions that, when placed back in to the sentence, make it correct. There is only one correct answer for this type of question.

An example fill in the blank question is

PHP is a general purpose _____ language that is mostly used for _____ and can be embedded in _____.

   A. Web, Web development, web pages

   B. scripting, Web development, HTML

   C. scripting, server-side development, JavaScript

   D. procedural, Web development, HTML

Open Questions

An open question is probably the most difficult question type where the examinee is requested to give text answers to the question. There are no choices here but just a text box for the answer. The majority of these questions will request a PHP function name (do not include the parentheses in the answer), where others might request the output of a code snippet or other PHP keywords.

An example open question is

What function in PHP is used to display an HTML output of the PHP configuration and setup?

        Answer: _____

Figure 13.3 shows an example of how an open question would appear in an exam.

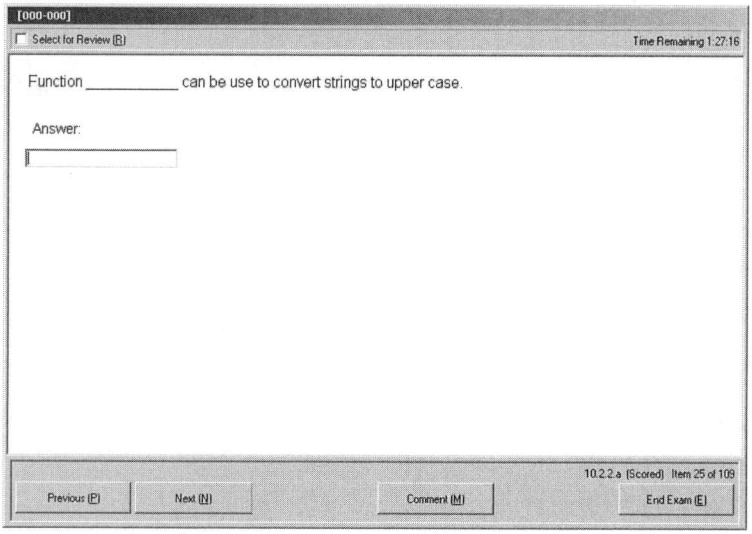

Figure 13.3   An open question.

Practice Exam Questions

1. Which of the following strings are not valid modes for the `fopen()` function?

    A. `a+b`

    B. `b+a`

    C. `at`

    D. `w`

    E. `x+`

2. Consider the following piece of code:

```php
<?php
$arr = array(3 => "First", 2=>"Second", 1=>"Third");
list (, $result) = $arr;
?>
```

    After running it, the value of `$result` would be

    A. `First`

    B. `Second`

    C. `Third`

    D. This piece of code will not run, but fail with a parse error.

3. In standard SQL-92, which of these situations do not require or cannot be handled through the use of an aggregate SQL function? (Choose 2)

    A. Calculating the sum of all the values in a column.

    B. Determining the minimum value in a result set.

    C. Grouping the results of a query by one or more fields.

    D. Calculating the sum of all values in a column and retrieving all the values of another column that is not part of an aggregate function or GROUP BY clause.

    E. Determining the mean average of a column in a group of rows.

4. Multidimensional arrays can be sorted using the _____ function.

5. When using the default session handler `files` for using sessions, PHP stores session information on the harddrive of the webserver. When are those session files cleaned up?

   A. PHP will delete the associated session file when `session_destroy()` is called from within a script.

   B. When the function `session_cleanup()` is called, PHP will iterate over all session files, and delete them if they exceeded the session timeout limit.

   C. When the function `session_start()` is called, PHP will iterate over all session files, and delete them if they exceeded the session timeout limit.

   D. When the function `session_start()` is called, PHP will sometimes iterate over all session files, and delete them if they exceeded the session timeout limit.

   E. Session files are never removed from the filesystem, you need to use an automated script (such as a `cronjob`) to do this.

6. What is the order of parameters in the `mail()` function?

   A. subject, to address, extra headers, body

   B. to address, subject, extra headers, body

   C. to address, subject, body, extra headers

   D. subject, to address, body, extra headers

7. Which of the following statements are correct? (Choose 3)

   A. `sprintf()` does not output the generated string.

   B. `printf("%2s%1s", "ab", "c")` outputs the string abc.

   C. `vprintf()` takes at least one parameter; the first parameter is the formatting string and the following parameters are the arguments for the '%' placeholders.

   D. `printf("%c", "64")` will output @ and not 6.

   E. `sprintf("%3.4f", $x)` outputs more than 7 characters.

   F. `number_format()` inserts thousands of separators and decimal points different from (,) and (.) respectively, while `printf()` like functions always use (.) as decimal point.

8. The requirement is to return `true` for the case in which a string `$str` contains another string `$substr` after the first character of `$str`? Which of the following will return `true` when string `$str` contains string `$substr`, but only after the first character of `$str`?

    I.
    ```php
    <?php
            function test($str, $substr) {
                    return strpos(substr($str,1), $substr) >= 0;
            \}
    ?>
    ```

    II.
    ```php
    <?php
            function test($str, $substr) {
                    return strrchr($str, $substr) !== false;
            \}
    ?>
    ```

    III.
    ```php
    <?php
            function test($str, $substr) {
                    return strpos($str, $substr) > 0;
            \}
    ?>
    ```

    A. I only
    B. II only
    C. III only
    D. I and II
    E. I and III
    F. II and III

9. Which of the features listed below do not exist in PHP4? (Choose 2)

    A. Exceptions
    B. Preprocessor instructions
    C. Control structures
    D. Classes and objects
    E. Constants

10. What is the output of the following code snippet?

```php
<?php
class Vehicle {
\}

class Car extends Vehicle {
\}

class Ferrari extends Car {
\}

var_dump(get_parent_class("Ferrari"));
?>
```

A. `string(7) "Vehicle"`

B. `string(3) "Car"`

C. `array(2) {`

```
            [0]=>
            string(7) "vehicle"
            [1]=>
            string(3) "car"
        \}
```

11. The following PHP script is designed to subtract two indexed arrays of numbers. Which statement is correct?

```php
<?php

$a = array(5, 2, 2, 3);
$b = array(5, 8, 1, 5);

var_dump(subArrays($a, $b));

function
subArrays($arr1,
        $arr2)
{
        $c = count($arr1);
        if
        ($c != count($arr2))
        return
null;
```

```
        for($i = 0;
                $i < $c;
                $i++)

                $res[$i]
                $arr1[$i] - $arr2[$i];

        return $res;

        \}
    ?>
```

A. The script is valid.

B. Assignments must be made on a single line.

C. It has too many linefeed characters between statements.

D. No, the script is missing curly braces.

E. Yes it is valid, but the script will not work as expected.

12. What is the purpose of the `escapeshellarg()` function?

   A. Removing malicious characters.

   B. Escaping malicious characters.

   C. Creating an array of arguments for a shell command.

   D. Preparing data to be used as a single argument in a shell command.

   E. None of the above.

13. The _____ function can be used to determine if the contents of a string can be interpreted as a number.

14. Assume `$comment` contains a string. Which PHP statement prints out the first 20 characters of `$comment` followed by three dots `(.)`?

   A. `print substr($comment, 20) . '...';`

   B. `print substr_replace($comment, '...', 20);`

   C. `print substr($comment, 20, strlen($comment)) . '...';`

   D. `print substr_replace($comment, 20, '...');`

15. What is the name of the function that you should use to put uploaded files into a permanent location on your server?

16. If you have a file handle for an opened file, use the _____ function to send all data remaining to be read from that file handle to the output buffer.

17. Which of the following sentences are not true? (Choose 2)

    A. `strpos()` allows searching for a substring in another string.

    B. `strrpos()` allows searching for a substring in another string.

    C. `strpos()` and `strrchr()` return -1 if the second parameter is not a substring of the first parameter.

    D. `strpos()` and `strrpos()` can return a value that is different from an integer.

    E. The second parameter to `substr()` is the length of the substring to extract.

    F. `strstr()` returns `false` if the substring specified by its second parameter is not found in the first parameter.

18. Which of the following sentences are correct? (Choose 2)

    A. `time() + 60*60*100` returns the current date and time plus one hour.

    B. `time() + 24*60*60` returns the current date and time plus one day.

    C. `time() + 24*60*60*100` returns the current date and time plus one day

Answers

1. B
2. C
3. C and D
4. `array_multisort` or `array_multisort()`
5. D
6. C
7. A, D, and F
8. C
9. A and B
10. A
11. B
12. D
13. `is_numeric` or `is_numeric()`
14. B
15. `move_uploaded_file` or `move_uploaded_file()`
16. `fpassthru` or `fpassthru()`
17. C and E
18. B

Glossary

Ad Hoc   To improvise solely in response to a particular situation and/or problem without considering wider issues.

Aggregate functions   Special SQL functions that take the values from multiple rows of data to produce a single result per grouping. Examples of aggregate functions include MIN(), MAX(), COUNT(), SUM(), and AVG().

API (Application Programming Interface)   A set of definitions by which a particular interface is accessed. The PHP API refers to the catalog of procedures and functions available for use from a userspace script.

Associative Arrays   An array indexed by associative (or string) keys. Array values are referenced by their "associated" key names.

ASP   Scripting environment provided by Microsoft for its IIS (Internet Information Services) web server in which HTML is combined with scripting and reusable ActiveX or .NET components to create dynamic web pages.

Array   A collection of data items identified by numeric and/or string indices. Arrays in PHP can also contain other arrays; an array that only contains other arrays is referred to as a multidimensional array.

Blocking and **nonblocking calls**   A blocking call is one that will "block" further execution of your script until conditions permit it to successfully complete or a predefined timeout occurs. A nonblocking call, by contrast, will fail immediately if it is not capable of completing its operation.

Boolean   An expression or variable that has two possible values: "true" and "false."

Bytecode   A meta language used by the PHP compiler to represent your script internally. Once your script has been converted to bytecode by the compiler, it will be passed to the executor to be run.

Bytecode cache   By default PHP will recompile your script into bytecode every time your page is requested whether the source code for your page has changed or not. A bytecode cache will compile your scripts once and reuse the bytecode until your script changes.

C   A programming language originally designed by Dennis Ritchie at AT&T Bell Labs in 1972 for systems programming on the PDP-11 and soon after used to re-implement UNIX. It was dubbed "C" because of the many features inherited from an earlier language named "B."

Class   A class definition is a prototype for an object in an object-oriented language defining member properties and methods for use within the class or object instantiation.

Client side   Any operation that occurs on the client's machine (usually within the context of a web browser). Typically, client-side operations are performed using JavaScript, Java Applets, Macromedia Flash, or ActiveX components. Client-side operations do not have direct access to server-side processes such as PHP.

Clone   Creates a copy of an object. In most cases, this simply means copying property values from the original object to the new object; however, cloning might require performing alteration or separation logic so that the new object does not create a resource conflict. In PHP 4, objects are cloned by default. In PHP 5, objects are implicitly referenced and only cloned by explicit request.

Column   Together with row defines a specific unit of information with a database table. All values within a given column describe the same type of information (that is, name, address, password, and so on). Columns are also referred to as fields.

Command Injection   A form of exploit attack, similar to SQL Injection, used against scripts that do not adequately validate or filter user supplied data. When unfiltered and unvalidated data is passed to a command-line function (`exec()`, `system()`, backtick operator, and so on), it can potentially allow a malicious user to execute arbitrary shell commands leading to disastrous results. See Chapter 11.

Constants   Similar to a variable except that it exists outside of variable scooping and can only be defined once. A constant's value cannot be changed once it is defined.

Cookie   A parameter supplied by the web server to the browser that the browser is expected to send back to the web server on its next visit. They can be set from PHP using the `set_cookie()` command and retrieved on next request in the `$_COOKIE` superglobal.

Cross-Site Scripting   Also known as XSS, this is a form of exploit attack in which a malicious user supplies content to be later displayed on your website (such as with a forum). This content is designed to fool other user's browsers into sending sensitive information to an untrusted target. See Chapter 11.

Data Validation   Scanning and sometimes filtering user supplied data to limit provided information to sensible constraints. This can be as simple as requiring an age field that only contains numbers, to as complex as ensuring that a URL is well formed and that the resource it refers to exists.

Database   A database is a generalized term for describing a logical grouping of data. Usually the term database will be used to refer to an RDBMS or a specific schema within an RDBMS.

Database indexing   A database index enables your RDBMS to more quickly find data based on identifying fields. For example, if you plan to allow searching by name, creating an index on the name field in your database will yield faster lookup results.

Date arrays   A compound representation of the current date and time using component values (month, day, year, hour, minute, second) contained in an array. Date arrays are used by a number of PHP functions, such as `gettimeofday()`.

Date Formatting Strings   Used with `date()` and `strftime()`, Date Formatting Strings contain a series of tokens along with ordinary string characters to translate a UNIX timestamp into a human readable date string.

Debuggers (DBG, APD, XDebug)
Debugger applications and extensions allow a developer to track the runtime execution of a script highlighting variable values and logic flow. Examples of debugging tools include DBG, APD, and XDebug. See Chapter 12.

Difference (Array Difference)   All elements that are unique to only one of two or more arrays. The result of calling `array_diff ()`.

Epoch   Midnight on January 1, 1970, in the UTC time zone. UNIX timestamps are measured as the number of seconds from this date.

Email   Electronic messages passed from one computer to another; this is often done across a network using SMTP and delivered locally using an MTA.

Error logging   Error logging (usually to a file) allows you as the site maintainer to keep a close eye on error conditions in your script. At the same time, this hides errors from your users who at best will not know what to do with the messages, or at worst will use those errors to compromise your site.

Escaping   Minor transformation on user supplied data used to avoid SQL and Command Injection attacks.

Exceptions   A runtime error reporting mechanism that provides a clean means of throwing and handling errors while preserving the environment stack.

File wrappers   A file wrapper defines how a specific implementation of a stream type should behave. Examples of file wrappers include the http:// and ftp:// wrappers, which implement specific protocols over network socket streams. See Chapter 10.

Foreign key   A special type of key that enforces Referential Integrity.

Function   A set of instructions that can manipulate the behavior of arguments passed and optionally return data to the calling scope. Functions that never return values are sometimes referred to as procedures.

GET method   The standard HTTP method for retrieving documents, web pages, and simple web application output from a web server. GET requests include the path and filename of the desired resource along with an optional set of request parameters passed with the URL. The maximum size of a GET request is determined by the HTTP specification of a URL length (currently 2,048 characters—including path and filename itself).

Grouping   Used with aggregate functions to combine data from multiple rows and/or multiple tables into complex results.

Hard-Coded   Data or values written directly into a program that cannot easily be modified during runtime.

Headers   A set of name and value pairs provided prior to email or HTTP content to define the constraints of the associated content. Examples of header names include `Content-Type`, `Content-Length`, `To`, `From`, `Subject`, `Content-Disposition`, `MIME-Version`, and others as defined by the specific transport syntax.

Heredoc   A string encapsulation format (similar to single and double quotes) that allows arbitrary delimiters. It is often used for interpolating variables within a very large string of data content.

HTML (Hypertext Markup Language)   Document format most commonly used on the World Wide Web.

HTTP (Hypertext Transfer Protocol)   The underlying application protocol used by web servers and browsers to request and transmit web pages and other documents. Refer to RFC 1945 and 2068 for more information.

Index   A collection of one or more key columns in a database table that organizes information for faster retrieval and updating.

Inheritance   Inheritance is the capability to derive new classes from existing ones. A derived class (also known as a child, or subclass) inherits the instance variables and methods from the base class (or a "superclass") and might add new instance variables and methods. New methods can be defined with the same name as those in the base class; if this is the case, the new methods will override those defined in the superclass.

Instantiation   Creating an object from a class definition.

Internal pointer   A psuedo-attribute common to all arrays in PHP. Initially this pointer looks at the first value in an array: Actions such as `next()`, `prev()`, `reset()`, and `end()` move the internal pointer forward, backward, and to the beginning and end of the array, respectively. The current key and value pointed to by an array's internal pointer can be accessed with `key()` and `current()`, respectively.

Interpreter   A program that compiles and executes human readable program code.

Intersection (Array Intersection)   All common elements of two or more arrays. The result of calling `array_intersect()`.

Key   Key columns are the components of indices that describe for the database how the information in a given table is organized. A database that is indexed on a given column is said to be "keyed" to that column.

MIME (Multipart Internet Message Extensions) Encoding   Originally defined by RFC 1341, MIME Encoding extends basic email encapsulation (which is limited to a single text body section) to allow for an arbitrary number of attachments—each of which might use a distinct content type and encoding.

MTA (Mail Transport Agent)   A piece of software that routes messages within a given host often providing an SMTP implementation and a sendmail wrapper.

Multidimensional arrays   An array that only contains other arrays.

Nesting   A form of logical grouping used with expressions and/or code blocks. Nesting helps define priority and functional process steps.

.NET (dot net)   A Microsoft supported API standard for language independent class interoperability. .NET is best showcased in C# but is supported by bindings from several languages including PHP.

Numeric arrays   An array indexed by numerical keys. Typically assigned sequentially from 0 upward and commonly accessed by an array walk or `for` loop.

Objects   Objects are collections of data and related code that support and act on that data. Objects in PHP, like most object-oriented languages, support inheritance, exceptions, and polymorphism.

Open Basedir   The `php.ini` setting `open_basedir` is a technique used on many Shared Hosting providers (along with `safe_mode`) to limit the ability of one user to read another user's files. When this setting is used, any running script is restricted from using `fopen()` or other filesystem access functions on files that reside outside the directory specified. However, on systems where arbitrary CGI scripts can be run or where the `exec()` family of functions is left enabled, the effectiveness of `open_basedir` is severely limited as any program or script written in another language might effectively bypass `open_basedir` restrictions. See Chapter 11.

Operators   Operators are symbolic expressions usually referring to mathematical tasks such as addition, subtraction, multiplication, and division.

Output   Data results transferred from a computer system to the outside world via some kind of output device such as a terminal or printer. In the case of PHP scripts, this usually refers to HTML sent to a web browser to be rendered as a web page.

Output buffering   Output buffering, controlled by settings in your `php.ini` or use of the `ob_start()` function, causes generated output to be temporary stored in memory. While generally streamlining the output pipeline, this process also enables an executing script to cancel, modify, or inject content even after "output" has already started. This also means that the `header()` command can be used after content has been output (normally not allowed).

Output caching   Often the output generated by a given page (report pages in particular) will be exactly the same over a period of time. An otherwise lengthy script run can be designed to output pregenerated content rather than repeating the same task over and over again. See Chapter 12.

Parsing   Parsing refers to the process by which program source code is broken into smaller, more distinct chunks of information that can be more easily interpreted and acted on.

Pass By Reference   Pass a variable to a function by first copying it. Any changes made to the passed variable from within the function will not affect the original value. This is the default behavior for function variables in PHP.

Pass By Value   Pass a variable to a function by creating a reference to it. Any changes made to the passed variable from within the function will be reflected in the original variable. This is done by placing an ampersand before the variable to be passed by reference within the function declaration.

PHP (PHP: Hypertext Preprocessor)
PHP is a server-side, cross-platform; HTML embedded scripting language most commonly used to create dynamic internet environments. Much of the language syntax is borrowed from C, Java, and PERL—with a unique flavor of its own. PHP was originally developed by Rasmus Lerdorf and then extended by Andi Gutmans, Zeev Suraski, and an assorted group of programmers from all over the world. PHP is distributed under the PHP license, which is a derivative of the BSD license and is considered an Open Source Project.

Primary key   A specific type of index used to uniquely identify a row in a database table.

Polymorphism   A property of object inheritance that enables methods of the same name to perform different actions through successive generations of a class definition.

POST method   The standard HTTP method for sending form content to a web server for online processing. A POST request is similar to a GET request except that the parameters (form data) are sent separately and have no hard limits on size (except those configured by the server administrator).

RDBMS (Relational Database Management System)   An RDBMS will contain one or more schemas (or databases)—each of which composes one or more tables with one or more columns (or fields) each.

Reference   A single variable in memory pointed to by two or more variable labels. If $a is a reference of $b, changing the value of $a will reflect in the value of $b and vice versa.

Referential Integrity   An assurance that the information between tables that relate to each other is self-consistent.

Register Globals   A sometimes controversial php.ini setting (register_ globals) that, when enabled, causes all data originating from GET or POST forms, as well as cookies, to be populated into the global scope. See Chapter 11.

Regular Expression (regex)   Regular expressions provide a robust language for specifying patterns in strings and extracting or replacing identified portions of text.

Resources   A special PHP variable type that refers to a more complex underlying data structure. Streams, database connections, and query result resources are the most common types of resources you'll encounter.

Row   A single record of data within a database table and uniquely identified by that table's primary key. Together with column identifies specific units of data.

Safe mode   The `php.ini` setting `safe_mode` is a technique used on many Shared Hosting providers (along with `open_basedir`) to limit the ability of one user to read another user's files. When this setting is enabled, a given script is only allowed to read files that are owned by the same user as the currently running script. However, on systems where arbitrary CGI scripts can be run or where the `exec()` family of functions is left enabled, the effectiveness of `safe_mode` is severely limited as any program or script written in another language might effectively bypass `safe_mode` restrictions. See Chapter 11.

Schema   One or more large structured sets of persistent data, usually grouped with other schemas within an RDBMS. A simple schema (or database) can be a file containing many records—each of which contains a common set of fields where each field is a certain fixed width.

Scope   Each function or object method maintains its own "scope" or variable stack—that is, `$foo` within a function is not the same variable as `$foo` outside a function. The exception to this rule are superglobals and constants that transcend scope and are equally available from any location within a script provided that they have been defined.

Script   A specific type of computer program that can be directly executed as source code by an interpreter program that understands the language in which the script is written. Scripts are typically compiled "on-the-fly" during each execution. Some languages, such as PHP, can be precompiled using a Bytecode cache.

Sendmail wrapper   A standard API, in the form of an executable program, used by most UNIX MTAs such as Sendmail, Postfix, Exim, Qmail, and Smail. PHP uses this wrapper when the `mail()` function is called and the `php.ini` value `sendmail_path` is defined.

Server side   Any operation that is performed on the web server prior to sending content back to the web browser (or client). PHP (similar to most CGI-based languages) is entirely server side. After the output has been generated and sent to the browser, PHP no longer has interaction with the client until a new request is made.

Session   A mechanism for persisting information between page requests from a particular user. After calling `session_start()`, data stored in the `$_SESSION` superglobal will continue to be accessible in future page requests from a client identified by a cookie, POST variable, or GET parameter.

SGML (Standard Generalized Markup Language)   The parent standards definition of both HTML and XML. SGML provides a foundation for defining syntactically compatible markup languages.

Shared Hosting   Command to many low-cost web service providers. A Shared Hosting server, as the name implies, is used by multiple unrelated parties who share limited, if any, trust. While offering attractive pricing, Shared Hosting opens the door to potential security risks, as unknown third parties might be able to gain access to sensitive information stored in your scripts, such as database passwords. See Chapter 11.

Serialization   Reformatting the contents of an array or object into a string value that can then be stored in a file or database.

SMTP (Simple Mail Transfer Protocol) Originally defined in RFC 821, the objective of SMTP is to transfer mail reliably and efficiently between remote servers on the Internet.

Sockets   A socket is an end point for a two-way communication stream. The most common use of sockets in PHP is for network communications using the INET socket family. Sockets can be opened as a stream using the `fsockopen()` function or as a socket resource using the sockets extension and the `socket_*()` family of functions. See Chapter 10.

Sorting   Reorganizing the output of a select query or array by the values in a given column or columns. See Chapters 4 (Arrays) or 9 (PHP and Databases).

SQL Injection   A form of exploit attack, similar to Command Injection, used against scripts that do not adequately validate or filter user supplied data. When unfiltered and unvalidated data is passed to a SQL query, it can potentially allow a malicious user to execute arbitrary SQL commands enabling him to steal and/or destroy important information. See Chapter 11.

Static method   An object method that, although it performs object related functions, does not require an object instance.

Streams   A stream is a generalized term for any sequential access input/output information pipeline. Examples of streams include ordinary files, network sockets, FIFOs, UNIX Domain sockets, character devices, or even blocks of memory. Regardless of type, all streams can be accessed using a common set of API calls known as the streams layer. These API calls include `fopen()`/`fsockopen()`, `fread()`, `fwrite()`, `fclose()`, `file()`, `file_get_contents()`, and many others. See Chapter 10.

String   A string is a sequence of characters that are considered as a single data element.

Structured code   A generalized term defining the organization of code into logical groups. This might refer to templating, which separates your application logic from your presentation layer, or the organization of your application logic into procedural and/or object-oriented groups.

Superglobal   A special internally defined variable that is always in scope. The standard complement of superglobals include $_GET, $_POST, $_REQUEST, $_COOKIE, $_SESSION, $_SERVER, $_ENV, $_FILE, and $GLOBALS. Each of these is an array; however, some might be empty if no related data is available.

Syntax   An orderly system and set of rules by which a programming language can be consistently interpreted and executed.

Table   A table is a logical unit within a database that describes one or more rows of data made up of one or more columns (or fields).

Templating   A process of separating code logic from presentation layer by embedding simple tokens within HTML content, and then allowing a template parser to replace the tokens with code and database driven content.

Ternary operator   The ternary operator is a shorthand version of an if/then/else statement. Three expressions are grouped as (condition) ? (if-true) : (if-false),. If the first expression is true, the second condition will be evaluated; if it is false, the third will be evaluated instead. See Chapter 12.

Transaction   A collection of one or more SQL statements that are to be committed to a database engine as a single atomic operation. Transactions help ensure data integrity by guaranteeing that either all, or none, of a given set of SQL statements will be processed.

UNIX timestamp   The standard for representing a date and time in most applications designed for POSIX compliant unixes including PHP. A UNIX timestamp is a measure of the number of seconds that have passed since the UNIX Epoch (Midnight, Jan 1, 1970 UTC).

UTC (Coordinated Universal Time) Also known as GMT (Greenwich Mean Time) and located along the prime meridian. UTC is the central time zone against which all other time zones are measured relative to.

Variable   A named memory location in which a program can store intermediate results.

Variable variables   The process of referring to a variable by a name that is determined at runtime.

Walking   Iterating through each of the elements of an array and applying a consistent set of operations to each element.

XML (Extensible Markup Language) An extremely simple dialect of SGML designed by the W3C with the specific purpose of serving, receiving, and processing SGML on the Web in a way similar to HTML. XML has been designed for ease of implementation, dynamic extension, and for interoperability with both SGML and HTML.

ZEND   The PHP language engine, named for its co-creators Zeev Suraski and Andi Gutmans, which handles the compilation and execution of PHP scripts as well as management of the PHP API.

Index

connecting remote hosts via sockets, 166–167

constants
creating via define ( ) construct, 14
function of, 14

context (streams), creating, 165

continue statement in loop structures, 28

cookies
headers, 54–55
session management, 56–57
transaction process, 54–55

Coordinated Universal Time (CUT), 116

copy( ) function, use with file wrappers, 163

copying files via fcopy( ) function, 110

count( ) function, 152
array elements, counting, 65

CREATE TABLE statement (DBMSs), 149

cross-site scripting (XSS), security issues, 180

D

data
arrays, 11
Boolean values, true/false conditions, 11
constants
creating via define ( ) construct, 14
function of, 14
containment via variables, 12
extraction via regular expressions, 100–101
forms, handling via superglobal arrays, 51–54
manipulation of, 9–12
NULL type, 11
numeric types
integer, 9-10
real, 9-10
operators, 14
arithmetic, 15
assignment, 14
associativity, 19-20
bitwise, 16
combined assignment, 19
comparison, 17-18
error-control, 16-17
logical, 18

precedence, 19-20
string, 17
typecasting, 19
resource values, 12
strings
extracting, 95-96
values, declaration methods, 10-11
variables, substitution in strings, 13

data filtering
blacklist approach, 178
whitelist approach, 178

database administrators (DBAs), indices optimization, 147

database management servers. See DBMSs

databases
data impurities, 153-154
date handling, 154
escape sequences, 153-154
indices
foreign keys, 148
good writing rules, 147
primary keys, 148
information, sorting (ORDER BY clause), 152-153
optimization measures
query limits, 195
table indexes, 195-196
resultsets, grouping, 151-152
shell command injections, security vulnerabilities, 180
SQL injections, security vulnerabilities, 179
table indices, 147

date arrays, 115
element keys, 116
retrieving, 117-119

date formats
date arrays, 115-116
string-formatted dates, 115-116, 119-123
UNIX time stamps, 115-116

date( ) function, formatting tokens, 119-120

DBMSs (database management servers), 145
escape sequences, 153-154
indices
foreign keys, 148
good writing rules, 147
primary keys, 148

G – H

P

POSIX regular expressions, 98
precedence rules (operators), 19-20
prefix decrementing (—) operator, 15
prefix incrementing (++) operator, 15
preg_replace( ) function, 101
preg_split( ) function, string splits, 101-102
primary keys (database indices), 148
printf( ) function
  family functions
    fprint( ), 95
    sprint( ), 95
    vprint( ), 95
    vsprint( ), 95
  format specifiers, 93-95
  strings, formatting, 93-95
processing forms via superglobal arrays, 51-54

Q - R

queries, limiting for database optimization measures, 195
questions (exam)
  fill-in-the-blank type, 207
  multiple choice type, 205-206
  open type, 207
  single choice type, 204-205

randomizing arrays, 81-82
read pipelines, 165
readfile( ) function
  files, reading, 112
  use with file wrappers, 163
reading
  files
    fread( ) function, 107
    readfile( ) function, 112
    single line at time (fgets( ) function), 107-108
    from sockets, 169
real numeric data types, 9-10
referential integrity, 148
register_globals directive, enabled dangers, 178-179
registering for Zend PHP Certification exam, 201-202

regular expressions (regexps), 98
  data extraction, 100-101
  pattern replacement, 101
  PCRE (Perl Compatible Regular Expressions), 98
    base character classes, 98-99
    enumerator operators, 99-100
    pattern modifiers, 100
  POSIX, 98
relational databases (schemas), 146
remote hosts, connecting via sockets, 166-167
rename( ) function, files, moving, 111
replacing
  patterns via regular expressions, 101
  substrings, 97-98
require construct, 8-9
require once construct, 8-9
reset( ) function, internal pointer, calling in arrays, 70-71
resource allocation, testing prior to code writing, 190-191
resource data values, 12
resultsets
  aggregate functions, 152
  grouping, 151-152
retrieving
  database information with SELECT statement, 150
  date arrays, 117-119
  file information via fstats( ) function, 109
  stream metadata, 164-165
  UNIX time stamp, 117
    from date arrays, 123
    from strings, 123-124
RFCs (Request for Comments)
  email standards, 140
  Internet Engineering Task Force (IETF), 172
ROLLBACK TRANSACTION command, 153
rows
  aggregates, 152
  tables
    deleting (DBMSs), 149-150
    inserting (DBMSs), 149
rsort( ) function, array sorts, 76-77

dollar sign ($) syntax, 13
function of, 12
scope, 30–31
script advantages, 13
strings, substituting, 13

W – Z

wake_up( ) function, object serialization, 44–45
walking through arrays, 68–71
Web browsers
error messages, displaying, 192–193
forms, processing, 51–54
HTTP requests, 50
web pages, output scripts, compression of, 195
web servers, performance optimization measures
child processes, 194
DNS resolution reversal, 194
websites
database optimization
query limits, 195
table indexes, 195-196
Internet Engineering Task Force (IETF), 172
Internet Mail Consortium, 140
Pearson VUE, 201
while statement in loop structures, 25–26
whitelist approach, data filtering, 178
whitespace in code writing, 186
Windows, email, sending, 131–132
write pipelines, 165
writing
code
command splitting over multiple lines, 188
flattening of if statements, 187-188
if statements, embedding, 191-192
logical groupings, 186
predefined standards, 186
program documentation, 186
tag styles, 189
testing for resource allocation, 190-191
use of concatenation operator, 188-189
use of condition statements, 189-190
use of identity operators, 190
whitespace, 186

to files with fwrite( ) function, 108–109
indices for databases, 147
to sockets, 169

XOR operator (logical), 18

Zend Performance Suite, 197
Zend PHP Certification, exams, registering, 201

Your Guide
to Computer
Technology

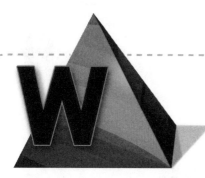

IT WON'T MAKE YOU SMARTER,

BUT IT'LL MAKE YOU A BETTER PHP PROGRAMMER.

php | architect is the Magazine for PHP Professionals. Every issue comes jam-packed with exciting new articles on practical topics from the best authors and programmers in the field. Here are some of the topics we tackled recently:

- Neural networks
- Smarty internationalization
- Database abstraction
- PHP 5, OOP and programming patterns
- Mastering regular expressions
- Extending PHP

Subscribe online today and save $5*
Simply enter promotion #32N5Y80288 when subscribing and get $5 US* off your purchase!

php | architect
The Magazine For PHP Professionals

www.phparch.com - (877) 630-6202